BARRON'S

EARLY ACHIEVER

GRADE 3

ENGLISH LANGUAGE ARTS WORKBOOK
ACTIVITIES & PRACTICE

REVIEW • UNDERSTAND • DISCOVER

Published by Kaplan North America, LLC, d/b/a Barron's Educational Series
1515 W. Cypress Creek Road
Fort Lauderdale, FL 33309
www.barronseduc.com

ISBN 978-1-5062-8154-4

10 9 8 7 6 5 4 3 2 1

Kaplan North America, LLC, d/b/a Barron's Educational Series print books are available at special quantity discounts to use for sales promotions, employee premiums, or educational purposes. For more information or to purchase books, please call the Simon & Schuster special sales department at 866-506-1949.

Introduction

Barron's Early Achiever workbooks are based on sound educational practices and include both parent-friendly and teacher-friendly explanations of specific learning goals and how students can achieve them through fun and interesting activities and practice. This exciting series mirrors the way English Language Arts is taught in the classroom. *Early Achiever Grade 3 English Language Arts* presents these skills through different units of related materials that reinforce each learning goal in a meaningful way. The Review, Understand, and Discover sections assist parents, teachers, and tutors in helping students apply skills at a higher level. Additionally, students will become familiar and comfortable with the manner of presentation and learning, as this is what they experience every day in the classroom. These factors will help early achievers master the skills and learning goals in English Language Arts and will also provide an opportunity for parents to play a larger role in their children's education.

Learning Goals for English Language Arts

The following explanation of educational goals is based on the skills that your student will learn in the third grade.

Reading Foundational Skills

Fluency

Your student will do/learn the following:

- Read on-level text with purpose and understanding
- Read on-level prose and poetry orally with accuracy, appropriate rate, and expression on successive readings
- Use context to confirm or self-correct word recognition and understanding, rereading as necessary

Reading Skills

Key Ideas and Details

Your student will do/learn the following:

- Ask and answer questions to demonstrate understanding of a text, referring explicitly to the text as the basis for the answers
- Determine the main idea of a text; recount the key details and explain how they support the main idea
- Describe the relationship between a series of historical events, scientific ideas or concepts, or steps in technical procedures in a text, using language that pertains to times, sequence, and cause/effect

- Recount stories, including fables, folktales, and myths from diverse cultures; determine the central message, lesson, or moral and explain how it is conveyed through key details in the text
- Describe characters in a story (e.g., their traits, motivations, or feelings) and explain how their actions contribute to the sequence of events

Text Structure

Your student will do/learn the following:

- Determine the meaning of general academic and domain-specific words and phrases in a text relevant to a grade 3 topic or subject area
- Use text features and search tools (e.g., key words, sidebars, hyperlinks) to locate information relevant to a given topic efficiently
- Distinguish his or her own point of view from that of the author of a text

- Determine the meaning of words and phrases as they are used in a text, distinguishing literal from non-literal language
- Refer to parts of stories, dramas, and poems when writing or speaking about a text, using terms such as chapter, scene, and stanza; describe how each successive part builds on earlier sections
- Distinguish his or her own point of view from that of the narrator or those of the characters

Analyzing Text

Your student will do/learn the following:

- Use information gained from illustrations (e.g., maps, photographs) and the words in a text to demonstrate understanding of the text (e.g., where, when, why, and how key events occur)
- Describe the logical connection between particular sentences and paragraphs in a text (e.g., comparison, cause/effect, first/second/third in a sequence)
- Compare and contrast the most important points and key details presented in two texts on the same topic
- Explain how specific aspects of a text's illustrations contribute to what is conveyed by the words in a story (e.g., create mood, emphasize aspects of a character or setting)
- Compare and contrast the themes, settings, and plots of stories written by the same author about the same or similar characters (e.g., in books from a series)

Writing Skills

Text Types and Purposes

Your student will do/learn the following:

- Write opinion pieces on topics or texts, supporting a point of view with reasons
- Introduce the topic or text, state an opinion, and create an organizational structure that lists reasons
- Provide reasons that support the opinion
- Use linking words and phrases (e.g., because, therefore, since, for example) to connect opinion and reasons
- Provide a concluding statement or section
- Write informative/explanatory essays to examine a topic and convey ideas and information clearly
- Introduce a topic and group related information together; include illustrations when useful to aiding comprehension
- Develop the topic with facts, definitions, and details

- Use linking words and phrases (e.g., also, another, and, more, but) to connect ideas within categories of information
- Provide a concluding statement or section
- Write narratives to develop real or imagined experiences or events using effective techniques, descriptive details, and clear event sequences
- Establish a situation and introduce a narrator and/or characters; organize an event sequence that unfolds naturally
- Use dialogue and descriptions of actions, thoughts, and feelings to develop experiences and events or show the response of characters to situations
- Use temporal words and phrases to signal event order
- Provide a sense of closure

Language Skills

Conventions of Standard English

Your student will do/learn the following:

- Explain the function of nouns, pronouns, verbs, adjectives, and adverbs, in general, and their functions in particular sentences
- Form and use regular and irregular plural nouns
- Use abstract nouns (e.g., childhood)
- Form and use regular and irregular verbs
- Form and use the simple (e.g., I walked; I walk; I will walk) verb tenses
- Ensure subject-verb and pronoun-antecedent agreement
- Form and use comparative and superlative adjectives and adverbs, and choose between them depending on what is to be modified
- Use coordinating and subordinating conjunctions
- Produce simple, compound, and complex sentences
- Capitalize appropriate words in titles
- Use commas in addresses
- Use commas and quotation marks in dialogue
- Form and use possessives
- Use conventional spelling for high-frequency and other studied words, and for adding suffixes to base words (e.g., sitting, smiled, cries, happiness)
- Use spelling patterns and generalizations (e.g., word families, position-based spellings, syllable patterns, ending rules, meaningful word parts) in writing words
- Consult reference materials, including beginning dictionaries, as needed, to check and correct spellings

Learning Goals for English Language Arts

Knowledge of Language

Your student will do/learn the following:

- Choose words and phrases for effect (requires additional attention in higher grades)
- Recognize and observe differences between the rules of spoken and written standard English

Vocabulary Skills

Your student will do/learn the following:

- Use sentence-level context as a clue to the meaning of a word or phrase
- Determine the meaning of the new word formed when a known affix is added to a known word (e.g., agreeable/disagreeable, comfortable/uncomfortable, care/careless, heat/preheat)
- Use a known root word as a clue to the meaning of an unknown word with the same root (e.g., company, companion)

- Use glossaries or beginning dictionaries, both print and digital, to determine or clarify the precise meaning of key words and phrases
- Demonstrate understanding of figurative language, word relationships, and nuances in word meanings
- Distinguish the literal and nonliteral meanings of words and phrases in context (e.g., take steps)
- Identify real-life connections between words and their use (e.g., describe people who are friendly or helpful)
- Distinguish shades of meaning among related words that describe states of mind or degrees of certainty (e.g., knew, believed, suspected, heard, wondered)
- Acquire and accurately use grade-appropriate conversational, general academic, and domain-specific words and phrases, including those that signal spatial and temporal relationships (e.g., After dinner that night, we went looking for them.)

Contents

Contents

Reading Foundational Skills

Fluency: Read with Purpose and Understanding

In this section, you will work with an adult as you practice and develop the art of fluent reading. Fluency means reading with speed, accuracy, and proper expression.

Fluency provides a connection between recognizing and understanding words. When reading quietly, fluent readers will group words together so that they recognize them right away. When reading aloud, they have a naturalness to their reading and speak with expression.

Whether you are a fluent reader already, or are working toward this goal, keep practicing so that you continue to grow in your reading abilities.

We hope you enjoy reviewing these important skills as you progress through your journey to excellence.

Let's practice!

Adults:

Time your student for one minute while reading aloud, and cross out any words that were eliminated or misread. At the end of one minute, mark the last word your student read and allow your early achiever to finish reading the text. Count the total number of errors and subtract that from the number of words read. This will give you the total number of words read per minute.

TOTAL NUMBER OF WORDS – NUMBER OF ERRORS = WORDS READ PER MINUTE

Over an extended period of time, your student's fluency should increase by the number of words read per minute.

Unit 2 (September)	Unit 4 (December)	Unit 6 (March)	Unit 8 (June)
90	100	105	115

The Family Camping Adventure

Last week, Tanya and Jason went camping with their mom. They drove for two long	15
hours just to get there. When they finally reached the park, they drove around for a very	32
long time looking for the perfect spot. It needed to be flat, have a place for a fire, and	51
have lots of trees. Jason yelled, "Mom, wait! That's the perfect spot." His mom agreed	66
and stopped the car.	70
Tanya, Jason, and their mom started to unpack the camping gear. Their tent was	84
shaped like a giant triangle. It was yellow and green and big enough for all three of	101
them. The tent was special because it had netting that went all the way around to keep	118
mosquitoes and other bugs from coming inside.	125
When it finally got dark, they built their fire. Their mom had a wonderful surprise	140
for Jason and Tanya. She had marshmallows, graham crackers, and chocolate bars.	152
Tanya jumped with joy. "Hooray, we're finally going to make **s'mores**!"	163

Words read in 1 minute – errors = WPM

CHECK FOR UNDERSTANDING

Adults: After your early achiever has finished reading, ask for a brief summary of the story so you can check comprehension. Write the summary on the lines below.

_____

_____

_____

GUIDED QUESTIONS

Use "The Family Camping Adventure" to answer the following questions.

1. Who finds the perfect spot for camping?

   _____

   _____

2. What does the tent look like, and what does it have that keeps bugs out?

   _____

   _____

3. How do Tanya and Jason feel about camping?

   _____

   _____

4. Reread the last two sentences of the story. What are **s'mores**? How does Tanya feel about eating them?

   _____

   _____

   _____

Good Friends

Good friends are hard to find. Marla wished she could rewind time so that she could	16
be nicer to her best friend. She had yelled at Amanda, "I don't want to be your friend	34
anymore!" Marla couldn't help it. She was **jealous** of Amanda. She was such a great	49
singer, and all Marla ever wanted to do was sing.	59
Marla began to cry. She could feel her tears slipping down her cheeks. Then she heard	75
a thump on her bedroom door. She looked up as her dog Tank came pushing in. Tank	92
hopped up on Marla's bed and began licking away her tears. Marla laughed a little at	108
Tank and his bad breath. Before she knew it, Marla was petting Tank's **broad** shoulders	123
and had forgotten she was sad. Tank's tail was wagging back and forth. Marla knew she	139
had made Tank happy.	143
Marla thought of Amanda and how she had treated her. Marla knew that a good	158
friend would say sorry and would explain why she chose to be so mean. She only hoped	175
that Amanda would forgive her.	180

Words read in 1 minute − errors = WPM

glossary

broad: Having a wide amount of space from one side to the other

jealous: Feeling dislike because of another person's talents

CHECK FOR UNDERSTANDING

Adults: After your early achiever has finished reading, ask for a brief summary of the story so you can check comprehension. Write the summary on the lines below.

_____

_____

_____

GUIDED QUESTIONS

Use "Good Friends" to answer the following questions.

1. What does Marla do to her friend Amanda?

_____

_____

2. What makes Marla laugh a little bit?

_____

_____

3. What does the author say to help you understand that Tank is happy?

_____

_____

4. Reread the first three sentences of the story aloud with expression. Does Marla appear to be angry with Amanda? How can you tell?

_____

_____

_____

Ready, Set, Dig!

Do you like to dig in the dirt and discover things that have been lost? How about | 17
locating items that have been underground for many years? If you do, you may be a | 33
future archaeologist! Archaeologists are scientists who study the past by digging and | 45
finding **fossils** and tools left by ancient people and animals. This cool science involves | 59
activities many kids love—digging in dirt and storytelling. Additionally, archaeologists | 70
are great at solving mysteries. When archaeologists find artifacts, or tools, they must | 83
think about how those artifacts arrived there and where they came from. | 95

The Digging Process | 98

Archaeologists have to look in certain places for artifacts. When they dig, they call this | 113
excavating. They use shovels, buckets, and large digging machines called bulldozers to | 125
find what they are looking for. | 131

About the Discovery | 134

What happens when artifacts are found? After archaeologists dig, they take what is | 147
found to a lab to study them. One artifact may tell the story of an entire group of people. | 166
For instance, archaeologists have found ancient toys from kids who were around the | 179
same age as you! By looking closely at the toys, scientists are able to tell what kids did for | 198
fun before there were televisions and electronic gadgets. | 206

Feeling Adventurous? Go on a Dig! | 212

Anyone can go on a dig. In fact, many archaeologists found their interest in digging when | 228
they were young kids. Imagine this: Thousands of years ago, people walked and lived on | 243
the same land that you live on today. Maybe you can **excavate** a small section of land in | 261
your backyard or neighborhood. Think about interesting places to dig, find a few tools, and | 276
see what's buried beneath the soil. Who knows what you'll find! If you do find an artifact, | 293
be sure to take it back to the lab and create a story of how you think it got there. | 313

Words read in 1 minute – errors = WPM

glossary

fossil: A trace or print of the remains of a plant or an animal

CHECK FOR UNDERSTANDING

Adults: After your early achiever has finished reading, ask for a brief summary of the story so you can check comprehension. Write the summary on the lines below.

_____

_____

_____

GUIDED QUESTIONS

Use "Ready, Set, Dig!" to answer the following questions:

1. Imagine you went on an archaeological dig. If you found an artifact, what would you do next?

_____

_____

2. If you like digging in the dirt at a young age, what could this mean?

_____

_____

3. Reread this sentence from the passage.

   "Maybe you can **excavate** a small section of land in your backyard or neighborhood."

   What does the word **excavate** mean? Use the other sentences in the passage to help you remember.

_____

_____

4. What is the purpose of this passage?

_____

_____

How to Play Checkers

Board games are a great way to spend time with a family member or a friend! Checkers,   17
which dates all the way back to ancient Egypt, is one of the oldest games known to   34
humankind. The rules of the game are quite simple. One player gets twelve red pieces,   50
while the other gets twelve black pieces. The goal is to do four main things to win: (1) Take   68
the other player's checkers from the board; (2) Get your checkers to the other person's   84
home row; (3) Position your checkers so that the other player has no available moves; (4)   100
Keep as many of your own checkers on the board as possible.   112

Here are step-by-step instructions on how to play: 122

1. Place the game board on a flat surface like a table or the floor.   137

2. Face the person you are playing with the board in between.   149

3. Each player chooses the color checkers to use.   158

4. Each person places checkers on the black squares in the three rows closest to   173
   the player. The row closest to each player is called the home row.   186

5. After deciding who will begin, the first player slides one of the checkers from one   202
   black square to another. The players take turns moving their checkers forward in a   216
   diagonal direction to the other side of the board.   225

6. When possible, players can jump over each other's checkers to land on a black   240
   square. This allows the person to win a checker and take it off the board.   255

7. When a player has finally reached the other person's home row, the player is crowned,   271
   by placing a checker on top of another checker of the same color. The crowned checker   287
   becomes a king. A king may be moved in any direction.   298

8. The game continues until one player has no more checkers on the board.   312

Words read in 1 minute – errors = WPM

CHECK FOR UNDERSTANDING

Adults: After your early achiever has finished reading, ask for a brief summary of the story so you can check comprehension. Write the summary on the lines below.

_____

_____

_____

GUIDED QUESTIONS

Use "How to Play Checkers" to answer the following questions:

1. How long have people been playing the game of checkers?

    _____

    _____

2. How does the author help the reader to understand how to play the game of checkers?

    _____

    _____

3. Reread this sentence making sure to use expression:

    "Board games are a great way to spend time with a family member or a friend!"

    Why does the author use an exclamation mark at the end of this sentence?

    _____

    _____

4. How does each player know that the game is finished?

    _____

    _____

    _____

Reading and Writing: Informational Texts

UNIT 2

American Athletes

Being able to read informational passages and understand their meaning is an important quality of a successful reader. In this section, you will read interesting passages on two famous athletes and will answer questions to show that you have understood what was read. You will also work on language-skills activities as well as fun writing exercises to complete each lesson.

Writing about informational texts will help to clarify what you know, what you have learned, and what you feel to be true, or your opinion.

Let's get started!

Babe Ruth—American Baseball Legend

1 Baseball can be a fun game to watch and play. When a person hits a home run, the fans get excited. A home run happens when the ball is hit and the batter runs all the bases in one play. The person who hits the most home runs often becomes the player that everybody likes to watch. In baseball history, one person held first place on the home run list for fifty-three years. His name was Babe Ruth. He became one of the most popular baseball stars of all time.

2 Ruth was born George Herman Ruth, Jr. on February 6, 1895, in Baltimore, Maryland. His parents sent him to an all-boys school because he often got into trouble. The boys' school was where Ruth first learned about baseball. He practiced how to throw and hit balls.

3 When Ruth was nineteen, the owner of the Baltimore Orioles, a **minor league** team, watched him play in a game. He was so impressed that the Orioles signed Ruth to a baseball **contract**. He looked so young that his teammates nicknamed him "Babe" or "Babe Ruth."

4 His first major league team was the Boston Red Sox. He soon became one of the best pitchers in baseball. But Ruth was admired even more for his hitting. As a pitcher, he could play only about two or three times a week. After the 1919 baseball season, his contract was sold to the New York Yankees. There, he became an everyday player in the **outfield**. As a result, he set home run records and had a high batting average. In 1920, he hit 54 home runs, more than any other player in the American League. During that season, over one million fans went to Ruth's home games in New York.

5 Ruth played with the Boston Braves in 1935 before he ended his baseball career. He hit a total of 714 home runs. Because he held the record for the most home runs, Babe Ruth was elected to the **Baseball Hall of Fame** in 1936.

glossary

Baseball Hall of Fame: An American history museum that honors people who have made great advances in the sport of baseball

contract: A written agreement

minor league: A group of players looking to someday become a part of the major leagues

outfield: The part of the baseball field beyond the infield and between the foul lines

Reading and Writing: Informational Texts

FINDING THE MAIN IDEA AND DETAILS

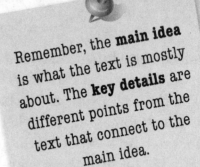

After reading "Babe Ruth—American Baseball Legend," answer the questions below.

*Remember, the **main idea** is what the text is mostly about. The **key details** are different points from the text that connect to the main idea.*

1. What is the **main idea** of the article?

   A. Ruth had behavior problems when he was young.

   B. Ruth received the name "Babe Ruth" from his teammates.

   C. Ruth was one of the most popular baseball players in history.

   D. Ruth began playing professional baseball at a very young age.

2. Which sentence **best** supports the main idea of the article?

   A. "There, he became an everyday player in the outfield."

   B. "His parents sent him to an all-boys school because he often got into trouble."

   C. "During that season, over one million fans went to Ruth's home games in New York."

   D. "When Ruth was nineteen, the owner of the Baltimore Orioles, a minor league team, watched him play in a game."

3. Explain why Ruth's career took off after playing for the New York Yankees. Be sure to use information from the text. Remember to use quotation marks when needed.

   _____

   _____

   _____

4. Which sentence is **most** important to include in a summary of this article?

   A. "Ruth played with the Boston Braves in 1935 before he ended his baseball career."

   B. "The boys' school was where Ruth first learned about baseball."

   C. "In 1920, he hit 54 home runs, more than any other player in the American League."

   D. "As a pitcher, he could play only about two or three times a week."

RELATIONSHIPS BETWEEN EVENTS

After reading the article "Babe Ruth—American Baseball Legend," use the chart below to fill in the events in the life of Babe Ruth showing a cause and effect relationship.

Cause is the REASON why something happens. **Effect** is the RESULT of what happened. Example: Babe Ruth's parents sent him to an all-boys school (RESULT) because he got into trouble. (REASON)

Cause	Effect
The Baltimore Orioles' owner came to watch Ruth play in one of his school's baseball games.	
Ruth became an everyday player in the outfield.	
	Over one million fans came to Ruth's home games in New York.
	Babe Ruth was elected to the Baseball Hall of Fame in 1936.

Digging Deeper

Batter Up!

Are you quick enough to hit a fastball? Most people react to a ball being thrown in two seconds. A ball traveling at 90 miles per hour will reach home plate in just half a second. If you were the batter, could you hit it in time? Try practicing hitting fastballs! Ask an adult to play with you. Record your reaction times and see how you can progress toward hitting the ball in half a second.

VERB TENSES

Verbs are divided into three main tenses: *past*, *present*, and *future*. Verb tenses tell the reader when the action is taking place.

The present tense tells readers the action is happening now. The past tense tells readers the action already happened. The future tense tells readers the action will happen later.

> $Example:$
>
> **Present Tense:** Jenny dances in the concert.
> **Past Tense:** Jenny danced in the concert.
> **Future Tense:** Jenny will dance in the concert.

Activity 1

Rewrite each sentence, changing the verb from the present tense to the future tense.

1. The player swings the bat.

   _____

   _____

2. The girl goes to the baseball game.

   _____

   _____

Activity 2

Read each sentence. Write *past*, *present*, or *future* after the sentence that contains a verb in each tense.

1. The boy caught the ball. _____

2. The coach will pitch the ball. _____

3. The team ran around the field. _____

4. The girl throws the ball over the fence. _____

USING COMMAS AND QUOTATION MARKS

Quotations are used to show a conversation between two or more people, which is called *dialogue*. Quotation marks (" ") are used before and after the speaker's words, with a comma inside the quotation mark. In other cases, a quote is set apart from the rest of the sentence by a comma.

Examples:

"I really did hit three home runs in one game," replied Darius.
(Comma inside quotations)

Susan said, "Please hand me the book."
(Comma sets quote apart from the sentence)

Add the missing quotation marks and commas to correctly punctuate the sentences.

1. George said I want to play baseball.

2. He hit a home run! screamed the coach.

3. She stated I would like to play baseball.

4. Can we go to the baseball field today? Todd asked.

5. Serena interrupted excitedly I know that we are going to win!

6. How old is your friend? asked the little girl. Old enough to play in the game said the little boy.

7. I saw the ball fly over the fence said Sunaya. How many times did that happen? asked Lelani.

Challenge: Write a few sentences in the past tense showing a conversation that Babe Ruth might have had with one of his fans. Be sure to place commas and quotation marks in the right places.

_____

_____

_____

A Champion Above the Rest

1   What is your favorite sport to play? If you spent time playing your favorite sport every day, how good would you become? A little girl named Serena Williams and her sister, Venus, grew up playing tennis. In fact, at one time, their father practiced with them for two hours every day! As a result, both sisters developed a deep desire to be great tennis players. Through much hard work, they have become respected women in the field of tennis around the globe. However, it is Serena Williams who has risen to be recognized as one of the greatest tennis players in the world.

2   Williams began tennis lessons when she was only three years old. By the time she was nine, Williams and her sister, Venus, went to special tennis schools where they learned how to play very well. They developed **power** and force as they practiced and became known for hitting balls at very fast speeds! The sisters soon became great tennis players.

3   Attending the special schools also gave them a chance to **compete** against other tennis players. When she was fourteen, Serena Williams entered her very first **professional tennis event**. Sometimes she won at these events, and other times she lost. Even when she lost a match, she held her head high. Williams always stayed positive and never gave up, which showed her great inner strength.

4   By the mid-1990s, both sisters had become professional tennis players. In 1999, Serena Williams was first in her family to win the US Open title. During the next ten years, Williams won twenty-three Grand Slam titles, including ten doubles championships with her sister, Venus. Their special style and abilities stood out from the other people who played against them. Together, the Williams sisters became good role models, especially for young African-American women, showing that success is possible with hard work.

5   By the time she was thirty-one years old, Williams had won a total of 641 tennis matches. Today, Serena has won a total of 39 Grand Slams, which in tennis is winning all four major championships—the championships of Australia, France, Britain (Wimbledon), and the United States—in the same calendar season. Williams's own personal tennis style, along with her ability to never give up, has not only changed her life, but also the world of tennis. She continues to be a wonderful example for athletes around the world.

glossary

compete: To play to win a prize or award against another person who is also trying to win the same prize

MAPPING THE MAIN IDEA AND SUPPORTING DETAILS

After reading "A Champion Above the Rest," use the graphic organizer to state the main idea and supporting details.

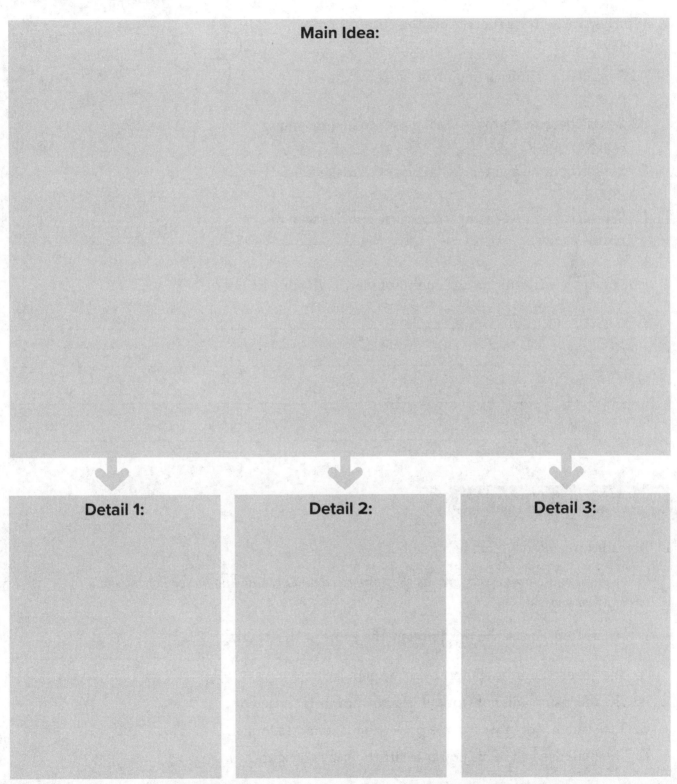

Main Idea:

Detail 1:

Detail 2:

Detail 3:

DIFFERENT POINTS OF VIEW

After reading "A Champion Above the Rest," answer the questions below.

By using all of the facts from the text, you will be able to determine how the author feels about the subject, or the author's **point of view**.

1. Which statement **best** describes the author's point of view?

    A. Serena is a tennis champion because she never gave up.

    B. Serena became a professional player to inspire young athletes.

    C. Serena became a professional player to make her father proud.

    D. Serena is a tennis champion because she has won many tennis games.

2. Do you agree with the author's point of view? Why or why not?

    _____

    _____

    _____

    _____

DETERMINING MEANING

1. Reread this sentence from paragraph 2.

    *"They developed **power** and force as they practiced and became known for hitting balls at very fast speeds!"*

    Which sentence uses the word **power** the same as in paragraph 2?

    A. The government has power over the people.

    B. The television will not work unless the power is turned on.

    C. The students do not have the power to make recess longer.

    D. The man used all of his power to lift the heavy weights.

2. Reread another sentence from paragraph 2.

   *"When she was fourteen, Williams entered her very first **professional tennis event**."*

   What does the phrase **professional tennis event** mean?

   A. A game where she competed against other players

   B. A fundraiser event to help support her tennis school

   C. A high school tennis game to prepare players for college

   D. A match where each player is one who earns a living playing tennis

VERB TENSES

The past tense of a verb shows that the action has already happened. Simply add an *-ed* to the present tense verb in order to change it to past tense. If a word already ends with an *e*, simply add a *d*.

dance ⤍ danced

walk ⤍ walked

Linking verbs do not express action, but they connect the subject of the verb to the additional information about the subject.

Devin *is making* a collage of his favorite sports.

When you are changing a verb from future to past tense, you will also need to drop the linking verb before changing the ending of a verb to make it past tense.

is making ⤍ is made ⤍ made

Irregular verbs do not follow the simple pattern of adding an *-ed* to the end of the word. Spelling can be tricky for these types of verbs. While some irregular verbs only change one letter, others have several letters that change. Memorizing is a great way to learn irregular verbs.

fly ⤍ flew

know ⤍ knew

spring ⤍ sprang

VERB TENSES

1. Rewrite the following sentences so that the verbs are written in the past tense.

   We **are watching** the World Tennis Championship on television.

   _____

   _____

   The player **will learn** a new way to hit the ball.

   _____

   _____

2. Change the following irregular verbs from present tense to past tense.

   A. ride _____

   B. buy _____

   C. become _____

   D. teach _____

VOCABULARY DEVELOPMENT AND USE

People often make connections between words and their own personal experiences. For instance, you know that someone who is friendly may also be kind. Who do you know in your own life who is friendly?

Use the word bank to fill in the blanks with the correct words from the text.

1. A(n)_____ is trained in exercise and sports.

2. Someone who keeps going when they want to quit

   has _____.

3. Performing a sport over and over until it becomes a skill requires

   _____.

4. A person who is strong may perform activities with _____.

word bank

athlete

force

inner strength

practice

Challenge: Using the words above, write a short paragraph identifying someone you know in real life who has one or more of these qualities.

_____

_____

_____

_____

_____

_____

_____

SPELLING PATTERNS

Some words have silent letters. The words **kn**ow, **wr**ap, **gh**ost, and **gn**aw have letters that we do not pronounce. Knowing these word patterns will help increase your understanding of the English language. It will also help you to write and speak properly.

Fill in each blank with a word that contains a silent-letter consonant pair (kn, wr, gh, or gn) as shown in the pictures.

1. Rafael skinned his _____ at summer camp.

2. The tennis match will be held late at _____.

3. Martina will _____ music for her song.

4. The _____ says that Serena Williams is playing tonight.

Challenge: Write three sentences using at least one word in each sentence that contains a silent-letter consonant pair. Underline the silent-letter consonant pair in each sentence.

Examples: My mother is <u>wr</u>apping Skylar's present.

_____

_____

_____

_____

WRITE YOUR OPINION

Serena and Venus Williams went to special tennis schools where they learned how to play very well. If they did not attend these schools, do you still think they would have become professional tennis players?

Write an opinion essay stating your answer. Be sure your essay has a topic sentence (or main idea) that tells your opinion. Next, list three reasons why you believe, or do not believe, that Serena and Venus would have become professional tennis players if they had not attended special tennis schools. Finally, write a conclusion that restates your opinion. Use the graphic organizer below to help you plan your essay.

Topic Sentence: _____

_____

_____

Reason 1: _____

_____

_____

Reason 2: _____

_____

_____

Reason 3: _____

_____

_____

Conclusion: _____

_____

_____

REVIEW

Reading Fluency

Adults: Time your student reading aloud for one minute. Make a note of where your student is at the end of one minute. (Your student should be able to read between 90 and 110 words per minute.) Have your student continue reading to the end of the passage in order to answer the questions below.

An Old Tradition Becomes New

Over 3,000 years ago, the Olympics, the world's most popular sports event, was created. In   15
ancient Greece, the Olympic games were held every four years in the summer to honor the   31
ancient Greek gods. It was a track and field competition that presented the best athletes.   46
This became the most famous out of all the sporting events in Greece.   59

They were held in a special area called Olympia that was located in the south of Greece.   76
For this reason, the games were named the Olympics. After many centuries, the Olympics   90
came to an end. The games that honored pagan gods were stopped for religious reasons by a   107
Greek ruler who worshipped a single God. Almost 1,500 years later, a French lord visited the   123
Olympic site in Greece. He supported physical education. The French lord became **inspired**   136
after his visit. He decided to start a modern Olympic program. The first modern Olympics   151
were held in Greece in the summer of 1896. Some of the events were track and field,   168
sprinting, swimming, cycling, and tennis. By 1924, the Winter Olympic games began. Ice   181
skating, ice hockey, and bobsledding were added to the sports lineup. In 2004, the Summer   196
Olympics once again took place in Greece. At this event, old traditions were combined with   211
new traditions. The **shot put** event was held at the very site where the original games in   228
Olympia were played. Shot put is a track and field event in which an athlete throws a heavy   246
object as far as possible.   251

Words read in 1 minute – errors = WPM

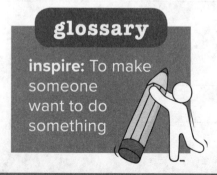

inspire: To make someone want to do something

Activity 1

Change each of the verb tenses in each sentence.

1. Many people watch the Olympics.

   Past: _____

   Future: _____

2. The instructor trains the students for the Olympic trials.

   Past: _____

   Future: _____

3. Jason and his two brothers take exercise classes at the YMCA.

   Past: _____

   Future: _____

4. My friend plays soccer in the 2012 Olympic games in London.

   Past: _____

   Future: _____

Activity 2

Correct the following sentences by placing commas and quotation marks where they are needed.

1. It's time to put your sneakers on said Dad.
2. Jamaeka replied One of the ancient Greek gods was named Zeus.
3. Are you going to enter the bicycle competition? asked the instructor.
4. The teacher told her students Take out your tennis rackets and begin practicing.

Activity 3

Think about words and their real-life connections. Then answer the questions.

1. A French lord was **inspired** to create the modern Olympic games after he visited the Olympic site in Greece. Describe an event or happening that **inspired** you to do something.

   _____

2. Describe the qualities a person would need to perform in the **shot put** event.

   _____

UNDERSTAND

Running Fast for Education

1 In the Summer Olympics of 2008 and 2012, the world was introduced to Usain Bolt. During these games, he earned the title, "The Fastest Man in the World." Bolt became an Olympic **legend** because of his amazing performances at these events.

2 Bolt is a sprinter. Sprinters move very fast at top speeds for a short time, as in the 100-, 200-, or 400-meter dashes. While growing up in the country of **Jamaica**, Bolt ran and won national track meets and became well-known by the age of fourteen. From 2001 to 2004, Bolt won many races in Jamaica running the 200- and 400-meter dashes. Finally, in late 2004, Bolt became a professional athlete.

3 When he arrived for the international competitions, Bolt had many people watching him to see what he could do. After winning a race, he became famous for his *Lightning Bolt* pose. For this reason and for his super fast feet, he quickly earned this nickname.

4 Bolt currently holds the world record in the 100-meter dash, finishing it in 9.58 seconds. He demonstrates his speed every time he races. In 2008, Bolt was the first man in history to win both the gold medals in the 100- and 200-meter dashes in the Olympics. In the 2012 Olympics, he kept both records and created new world records.

5 In addition to being an amazing athlete, Bolt is also a **humanitarian**. He is focused on improving the lives of other people. In his home country of Jamaica, he started the Usain Bolt Foundation.

6 In Jamaica, children do not have as many programs available to them as do those in other countries. As a result, this foundation works to help children by creating opportunities through education.

7 Throughout his career, Bolt has won many awards and earned many medals. However, his biggest wish is to remind children to "Dare to Dream" so that they, too, can do something wonderful with their lives.

glossary

Jamaica: An island in the Caribbean Sea

legend: An important person who becomes famous for doing something very well

After reading "Running Fast for Education," answer the questions below.

1. In the space below, write the **main idea** of the article.

    _____

    _____

2. List **two details** that support the main idea of the article.

    _____

    _____

3. How did Usain Bolt earn the *Lightning Bolt* nickname?

    _____

    _____

4. What is another possible title for this article?

    _____

    _____

5. Reread paragraph 5. What does the word **humanitarian** mean?

    A. A person who helps other people

    B. A person who dreams for other people

    C. A person who learns from other people

    D. A person who competes with other people

6. Reread this sentence from paragraph 1.

    *"Bolt became an Olympic **legend** because of his amazing performances at these events."*

    What information from the article supports the idea of Usain Bolt being a **legend**?

    _____

    _____

DISCOVER

Explanatory Writing

Think about the many different kinds of sports that exist. Which one do you especially find fun or interesting?

Sport

_____

Pick your favorite sport and do a little research with the help of an adult. Use the graphic organizer below to jot down what you learned about the sport. Then write an explanatory essay telling others all about that sport.

The sport I chose to write about is _____

Fact 1
Fact 2
Fact 3
Fact 4
Fact 5

Remember to use your *My Journal* pages at the back of the workbook if you need more space to write.

Introduce your topic: _____

_____

_____

_____

_____

_____

Use facts and definitions to develop your story and include drawings or diagrams:

_____

_____

_____

_____

_____

_____

_____

_____

_____

_____

_____

Write your conclusion: _____

_____

_____

_____

_____

_____

_____

Migration

Watching the movement, or migration, of animals is truly amazing. It is wonderful to see thousands of monarch butterflies roosting in trees or flocks of birds lining the skies flying south. For these insects and animals, migration is important to their survival. In this unit, you will learn about the biggest, longest, and most amazing animal migrations. You will understand why and how these creatures make their journeys, as well as some of the challenges they face along the way.

Happy reading!

Digging Deeper

Watch and Track Those Migrating Birds!

Research different kinds of birds that migrate to or from your area and create a map showing the birds' migratory path!

Up and Away!

1   Look into the sky in the fall or spring, and you may see a V-shaped flock of geese on the move. These geese are migrating, or moving from one location to another.

2 **Why Are Birds on the Move?**

Birds migrate for two main reasons: to find food and to find nesting locations. In the north, cold winter temperatures kill the worms and insects that birds eat. For this reason, birds have to fly south in the fall. In the spring, birds may migrate north where there are many places to lay their eggs, as well as plants and insects to eat.

Parent birds must find food to feed their hungry babies.

3 **Types of Migration**

There are three different kinds of bird migration: short, medium, and long. During short migration, birds travel short distances, such as from the top of a mountain to the bottom to find food. Medium migration means that birds will travel across one, two, or several states. During long migration, birds may **travel** thousands of miles, such as from the Northern United States to Mexico.

4 **When to Hit the Sky**

How do birds know when it is time to **hit the sky**? Birds know when to migrate by observing their environment. In the fall, the weather cools down and the days become shorter. It is also harder for birds to find food.

5 **Migration Paths**

How do birds know which path to take? They look for familiar landmarks, such as mountains, rivers, and even buildings. Day flyers, such as hawks and swallows, use the position of the sun as a kind of compass to **guide** their paths. Birds that fly at night, such as songbirds, can tell what direction they are flying by using the locations of stars. Birds' nostrils have a special mineral that allows them to use Earth's magnetic field to tell what direction is north.

6 **Migration Problems**

Birds, like humans, may run into problems while traveling. Dealing with bad weather and hunters can be challenging to birds during migration. In addition, they have to be on the lookout for predators and other birds or animals that may want to eat them. Finally, millions of birds are killed each year because they are attracted to lights and crash into tall buildings or towers.

UNDERSTANDING VOCABULARY

After reading "Up and Away!," answer the questions below.

1. What is the ***best*** meaning of the word **travel** in paragraph 3?

   A. To fly in the air for several hours

   B. To stay in one place for a long time

   C. To move from one place to another

   D. To move quickly without stopping

2. Read this sentence from the article.

   *"Day flyers, such as hawks and swallows, use the position of the sun as a kind of compass to **guide** their paths."*

   Which sentence uses the word **guide** the same as it is used in the sentence above?

   A. The tour guide led the people through the cave.

   B. The study guide will help the students pass the test.

   C. The map will guide the men to the right road.

   D. Every dictionary entry has guide words.

3. What does the phrase **hit the sky** mean?

   A. It is time to migrate.

   B. It is time to look at the sky.

   C. Birds should leave their nests.

   D. A group of birds should make a V shape.

DESCRIBING RELATIONSHIPS

Activity 1

Birds' migration habits depend on different factors, such as where they live and the present conditions within their environment. In the spaces below, tell which type of migration is being described.

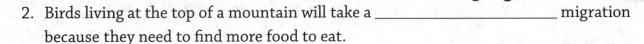

> Remember: **Cause** is the REASON why something happens. **Effect** is the RESULT of what happened. Example: The bird is safe because my brother saved it when its nest fell out of the tree.

1. Birds living in Alaska will take a _____ migration because they need to escape the cold winter.

2. Birds living at the top of a mountain will take a _____ migration because they need to find more food to eat.

3. Birds living in New York City will take a _____ migration northward so that they can find places to have their babies.

Activity 2

How much did you learn about migration? For each effect, list a relating cause. Fill in the chart below.

Cause	Effect
	1. Birds must migrate.
	2. They crash into buildings and towers.
	3. They use the Earth's magnetic field to tell which direction is north.

Reading and Writing: Informational Texts

UNDERSTANDING TEXT FEATURES

After reading "Up and Away!," answer the questions below.

1. What are the boldface titles in the article called?

    A. captions

    B. key words

    C. hyperlinks

    D. subheadings

2. Under which section can the reader find the reasons why birds migrate?

    A. Why Are Birds on the Move?

    B. When to Hit the Sky

    C. Migration Paths

    D. Migration Problems

3. Read the sentence below.

    "Nighttime lightning may stun birds while they are migrating."

    Under which subheading would this sentence appear if it were included in the article?

    A. Why Are Birds on the Move?

    B. When to Hit the Sky

    C. Migration Paths

    D. Migration Problems

4. What does the caption from the article tell the reader?

    _____

    _____

    _____

    _____

UNDERSTANDING PRONOUNS

Pronouns are used to take the place of a noun. Pronouns include *I, me, he, she, it, you, they, we, her, them, him,* and *us.*

Examples:

Noun	Pronoun
Cassie went to the pet store.	**She** went to the pet store.
The pet store was closed.	**It** was closed.
The children fed the parrots.	**They** fed the parrots.

Activity 1

Write the correct pronoun on the line to replace each noun.

1. Jeff's report on bird migration was so good that the teacher gave _____ an award. (her, him, their)

2. The boys saw baby sparrows outside _____ window. (his, her, their)

3. Birds must migrate to find food for _____ young. (its, they, their)

4. When Mr. Chen, the conservation officer, visited our class, _____ learned that birds know when to migrate by changes in temperature. (she, he, we)

Activity 2

Write the correct pronouns on the lines to replace the nouns in the paragraph.

My brother and I watched the geese flying with _____ binoculars. _____ are really interested in the migration of birds. Our teacher taught _____ some cool facts about migration last year. We learned that birds know the right flight path to take when _____ are migrating. They use the sun and stars to help guide _____.

TYPES OF SENTENCES

A **simple sentence** is a sentence with only one subject and predicate and one complete thought.

Example: The bird sang a pretty song.

A **compound sentence** is a sentence with two or more complete thoughts that are joined by a comma and words that connect the sentence parts (a conjunction), such as *or, but, and,* or *so.*

Example: I like to watch the flamingos, but I would rather feed the seagulls.

A **complex sentence** has a complete thought joined by one or more incomplete thoughts or sentences. A complex sentence always contains a pronoun, such as *who, that,* or *which,* or subordinating conjunctions, such as *when, since,* or *because,* that join the sentences together.

Example: Because the girls went on a bird-watching trip, they did not go to the library.

Activity 1

Write *simple, compound,* or *complex* on the line after each kind of sentence.

1. We saw the geese flying in the sky, and then they were gone. _____

2. Since the bird needed to find food for her babies, she migrated south. _____

3. The beautiful hawk flew south for the winter. _____

4. When the days get shorter, birds know it is time to move on. _____

5. Birds face many dangers while migrating, and many do not survive. _____

Activity 2

Write a simple, a compound, and a complex sentence on the following lines and label the simple sentence with S, the compound sentence with C, and the complex sentence with CP.

1. _____

2. _____

3. _____

A Butterfly Above the Rest

1 Imagine something that weighs less than an ounce with a brain no bigger than the head of a pin. It travels over 2,500 miles in six to eight weeks without getting lost! This would be impossible, unless you were a monarch butterfly. Monarch butterflies are insects that migrate, or move to different places. They travel from North America to Mexico every fall. No other insect on Earth migrates farther than the monarch.

2 There are different reasons why butterflies move. Weather changes and having babies will cause them to look for new locations. In the winter, monarch butterflies travel to Mexico to escape the cold. In the spring, they fly back north where there are many milkweed plants on which they can lay their eggs.

3 When monarchs lay their eggs on milkweed plants, a poison is released that keeps enemies away. The eggs hatch on the milkweed, and the larvae feed on the milkweed's leaves. Larvae then become caterpillars and enter the pupa stage. The caterpillars create a hard case around themselves. After a little while, the caterpillars become butterflies. However, scientists worry that monarchs may **disappear** someday. The poisons that farmers put on their fields are killing the milkweed plants.

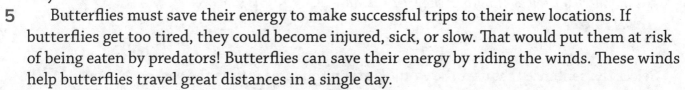

4 As monarch butterflies migrate, they use certain travel **routes**. Mountains and waterways become their guides. Butterflies **avoid** certain features of the Earth that may be dangerous for them. For example, traveling butterflies may not be able to fly over tall mountains. Instead, they will travel in between tall mountains to stay safe.

5 Butterflies must save their energy to make successful trips to their new locations. If butterflies get too tired, they could become injured, sick, or slow. That would put them at risk of being eaten by predators! Butterflies can save their energy by riding the winds. These winds help butterflies travel great distances in a single day.

DETERMINING MEANING

After reading "A Butterfly Above the Rest," answer the following questions.

1. What is the meaning of the word **disappear** in paragraph 3?

   A. move away

   B. die out

   C. travel far

   D. go into hiding

2. Read the following sentence from the article.

   *"Butterflies **avoid** certain features of the Earth that could be dangerous to them."*

   What is the meaning of **avoid** in the sentence above?

   A. move closer to

   B. stay away from

   C. look out over

   D. pay no attention to

3. Read the following sentence from the article.

   *"As monarch butterflies migrate, they use certain travel **routes**."*

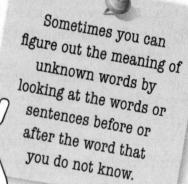

What happens when you come across a word that you don't understand?

Sometimes you can figure out the meaning of unknown words by looking at the words or sentences before or after the word that you do not know.

   Select the sentence that uses the word **route** in the same way as the sentence above.

   A. The bus driver took the shortest route to get to the beach.

   B. The teacher had to route my lunch form to the guidance counselor.

   C. My older brother works on a newspaper route in his new after-school job.

   D. The museum guide had to route our tour group through a new section of the building.

DESCRIBING CONNECTIONS

1. Which statement from the passage is explained by the information in paragraph 3?

   A. No other insect on earth migrates farther than the monarch.

   B. In the winter, monarch butterflies travel to Mexico to escape the cold.

   C. Butterflies avoid certain features of the Earth that may be dangerous for them.

   D. In the spring, they fly back north where there are many milkweed plants on which they can lay their eggs.

2. Read these sentences from the article.

   "The eggs hatch on the milkweed, and the larvae feed on the milkweed's leaves. Larvae then become caterpillars and enter the pupa stage."

   Which statement describes the relationship between these two sentences?

   A. The sentences make a comparison.

   B. The sentences describe three steps in a process.

   C. The first sentence explains the reason for the second.

   D. The second sentence gives the cause of the first sentence.

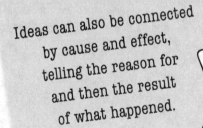

Ideas can be connected by comparing one to another to see similarities or differences. Or they may be the steps in a sequence: First, Second, Third.

Ideas can also be connected by cause and effect, telling the reason for and then the result of what happened.

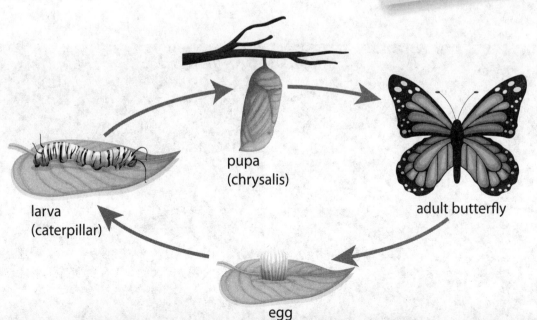

larva (caterpillar)

pupa (chrysalis)

adult butterfly

egg

COMPARING AND CONTRASTING ARTICLES

After reading "Up and Away!" and "A Butterfly Above the Rest," describe how the articles are similar and different. Fill in the Venn diagram below.

Snow Geese (different)

Same

Monarch (different)

USING SUFFIXES

A **suffix** is a group of letters added to the end of a word to create a new word. Adding a suffix will change the tense, meaning, or word type completely.

Activity 1

Combine a base word with a suffix from the chart below. Write each new word on the line below. (Each suffix can only be used once.)

Base Word	Suffix
butterfly	-ies
slow	-ied
try	-ed
injure	-ing
cloud	-ly
move	-y

1. _____
2. _____
3. _____
4. _____
5. _____
6. _____

Activity 2

Look at the following suffixes and their meanings. Write at least one word with each suffix on the lines below.

1. -less = without   Your word: _____

2. -ness = condition or state of   Your word: _____

3. -ing = action process   Your word: _____

PREFIXES OR SUFFIXES

A prefix or a suffix can be added to the beginning or the end of a root word in order to change its meaning. Prefixes are added to the beginning of words. Suffixes are added to the end of words.

Circle the correct definition for the underlined words below.

1. The monarchs traveled in a **cloudless** sky.

    (full of clouds, without clouds)

2. My sister made **arrangements** to visit the butterfly museum.

    (plans, selections)

3. The butterfly eggs were **carefully** placed on the milkweed.

    (very quickly, very gently)

4. The boy stood **motionless** when he saw thousands of butterflies in the field.

    (without motion, moving slowly)

5. Logan was **thoughtless** when he spilled paint on the milkweed plants.

    (not thinking, being unkind)

Challenge: Use each prefix from the box to create a word. Use the new word in a sentence. Then tell what the word means.

Prefix		Meaning
in-	--->	not
dis-	--->	not/opposite of
pre-	--->	before

1. Your word: _____ Meaning: _____

    Sentence: _____

2. Your word: _____ Meaning: _____

    Sentence: _____

3. Your word: _____ Meaning: _____

    Sentence: _____

WRITE YOUR STORY

A good story has three parts: characters, a setting, and a plot. A narrative uses these elements to describe actions, thoughts, and feelings. The plot of a narrative tells what happens. The conclusion is the ending that summarizes the plot, or what you wrote about in your story.

Imagine you are a monarch butterfly migrating from the United States to Mexico. Write about the journey and the troubles you find along the way. Be sure your story has characters, a setting, and a plot, as well as a conclusion.

Characters	Setting	Plot
Who is the story about?	When and where does the story take place?	What are the events in the story?
Have at least two main characters identified.	Is it summertime? Wintertime?	What adventures await your characters?
	What state or country will you choose?	Use your imagination!

Create a plot:

What happens first . . . _____

_____

Next . . . _____

_____

Then . . . _____

_____

Finally, how does your story end? Bring your story to an end by connecting the main points together through a well-thought-out conclusion. Use your imagination and have fun!

_____

_____

_____

_____

Nutrition and Exercise

This unit discusses some of the ways you can keep your body fit and healthy. You will read about nutrition, which refers to the types of foods you choose to eat and how your body uses the vitamins and minerals within the food. You will also learn about exercise, which refers to the physical activity you do with your body, like running or walking. Both eating right and exercising on a regular basis can help you feel happy and relaxed. They can even improve your ability to learn new things!

Happy reading!

Vitamin B
For energy and a healthy nervous system

Vitamin D
For strong bones, teeth, and gums

Vitamin A
For healthy skin and eyes

Vitamin E
For healthy red blood cells

Vitamin C
For a healthy immune system

Vitamin K
For normal blood clotting

Healthy Eating

1   Do you know some of the most important things that your body must do every day? Think about it. Each day your body is fixing itself and making new cells so that you can grow and be healthy. What you eat has a big effect on how well your body can do these things, and how healthy you will be.

2   Eating good food gives you energy, makes you grow big and strong, and helps your body heal if you get hurt or become sick. Your body needs nutrients from the food you eat. Did you know that some types of food are better for you than others? Foods that **contain** too much added sugar, as well as some fried foods, have little or no nutrients. To avoid the risk of developing health problems, it is important to make healthy food choices.

3   Before eating, do you think about the kind of food you will put on your plate? You should. The government has created a diagram called *MyPlate*. MyPlate explains how to build a healthy plate using the five main food groups: fruits, vegetables, grains, protein, and dairy.

4   Look at the following list of nutrients. It shows some important vitamins, the foods that contain them, and how they **benefit** the body.

5   Vitamin A keeps your skin and eyes healthy. You can get plenty of vitamin A by eating dark green and orange vegetables, such as spinach, asparagus, sweet potatoes, and carrots.

Vitamin D helps your body **absorb** calcium, which is a mineral found in milk, fish, liver, and eggs, that makes your teeth and bones strong. Vitamin D also plays an important role to help your body fight off germs. Your body can produce its own vitamin D from being out in the sun. It is sometimes called the *sunshine vitamin*.

Vitamin E, found in whole grains, wheat germ, and leafy green vegetables, helps your body **produce** red blood cells and keeps these cells healthy.

Vitamin C is found in several fruits and vegetables, such as oranges, tomatoes, peppers, broccoli, and cabbage. This vitamin keeps your gums and blood vessels healthy and your immune system strong.

Vitamin B, found in green vegetables, meat, and whole grains, helps your cells turn fat into energy, reduces the risk of heart disease, and helps your brain to stay strong and healthy.

Vitamin K is found in dark green vegetables, such as broccoli, kale, and asparagus. It is also found in milk, cabbage, and cauliflower. It is necessary for strong bones and normal blood clotting, so that you will not bleed too much if you get a cut or a scrape.

6   In addition to vitamins, you also need minerals, such as iron, calcium, copper, magnesium, potassium, and zinc. These and other minerals are also found in foods from each of the five food groups.

7   Reading nutrition labels can help you determine which foods are healthy. Nutrition labels list the amount of vitamins, minerals, calories (energy), and other ingredients that are contained within the food, and are found on all packaged food products.

UNDERSTANDING CONNECTIONS

After reading the article "Healthy Eating," complete the following activity. In the left column you will list each vitamin described in the passage. In the column on the right, you will list at least one benefit that it has for your body.

Vitamins	Benefits to Your Body
1.	
2.	
3.	
4.	
5.	
6.	

DETERMINING MEANING

After reading "Healthy Eating," answer the questions below.

1. Read this sentence from the article.

   *"Vitamin D helps your body **absorb** calcium, which is a mineral found in milk, fish, liver, and eggs, that makes your teeth and bones strong."*

   Which word(s) could replace the word **absorb** in the sentence above?

   A. adapt

   B. adjust

   C. take in

   D. take over

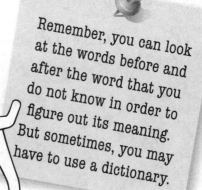

Remember, you can look at the words before and after the word that you do not know in order to figure out its meaning. But sometimes, you may have to use a dictionary.

2. Reread paragraph 4. What word could be used to replace the word **benefit**?

   A. help

   B. warm

   C. shape

   D. weaken

3. Which sentence has the same meaning for the word **contain** as in paragraph 2?

   A. The animal trainer had to contain the fierce lion.

   B. The book will contain important events in history.

   C. The joke was so funny, Jenny could not contain her laughter.

   D. The hospital must contain the disease to prevent it from spreading.

4. Read this sentence from the article.

   *"Vitamin E, found in whole grains, wheat germ, and leafy green vegetables, helps your body **produce** red blood cells and keeps these cells healthy."*

   Which word means the same as **produce** as it is used in the sentence above?

   A. give

   B. make

   C. take in

   D. get rid of

PICTURES HELP WITH UNDERSTANDING

Look at the two food nutrition labels to answer the questions below.

1. What percentage of vitamin A does nutrition label 2 have?

    A. 2%

    B. 5%

    C. 10%

    D. 25%

2. Which nutrition label is higher in fat grams, and what is the total amount?

    _____

    _____

    _____

3. Which important vitamin or mineral is found in nutrition label 1 that is not in nutrition label 2?

    A. Protein

    B. Iron

    C. Calcium

    D. Vitamin D

4. Which nutrition label would be the healthier choice? Explain why.

    _____

    _____

    _____

Nutrition Label 1

Nutrition Facts

Serving size: 1 bar
Serving per Container: 1

Amount Per Serving

Calories: 271	Calories From Fat: 122	
		% Daily Value *
Total Fat	13.6 g (grams)	
Cholesterol	7mg	2%
Sodium	140 mg	6%
Total Carbohydrates	34.5 g	12%
Dietary Fiber	1.3 g	5%
Sugars	26.6 g	
Protein	4.3 g	

Vitamins and/or Minerals (most to least):

Vitamin A, 2%	Vitamin C, 0%
Calcium, 5%	Iron, 2%

First 3 Ingredients:
1. Corn syrup
2. Sugar
3. Ground roasted peanuts

Nutrition Label 2

Nutrition Facts

Serving size: 1 Cup
Serving per Container: 1

Amount Per Serving

Calories: 120	Calories From Fat: 45	
		% Daily Value *
Total Fat	5 g (grams)	
Cholesterol	Less than 25 mg	8%
Sodium	120 mg	5%
Total Carbohydrates	20 g	7%
Dietary Fiber	0 g	0%
Sugars	11 g	
Protein	8 g	16%

Vitamins and/or Minerals (most to least):

Vitamin A, 10%	Vitamin C, 2%
Vitamin D, 25%	Calcium, 30%
Iron, 0%	

First 3 Ingredients:
1. Grade A reduced fat milk
2. Vitamin A Palmitate
3. Vitamin D3

DIFFERENT TYPES OF ADJECTIVES

There are different rules to learn about using adjectives.

Example:

Comparative adjectives compare one noun to another, such as *the car is faster than the truck*. We make adjectives comparative by adding *-er*, or for adjectives ending in a "y" by adding *-ier*.

Superlative adjectives compare three or more nouns and show which is best, such as *cold, colder,* and *coldest*. Review the following rules for making adjectives superlative:

1. One-syllable adjectives
   Comparative: add *-er* (older)
   Superlative: add *-est* (oldest)

2. Adjectives that are one syllable and end in "e"
   Comparative: add *-r* (braver)
   Superlative: add *-st* (bravest)

3. Adjectives that are one syllable and end in consonant–vowel–consonant
   Comparative: add consonant + *-er* (bigger)
   Superlative: add consonant + *-est* (biggest)

4. Adjectives ending in "y"
   Comparative: replace "y" with *-ier* (happier)
   Superlative: replace "y" with *-iest* (happiest)

Activity 1

Underline the word that *best* completes the sentence.

1. Fruits and vegetables are _____ than pies and cakes.
   (healther, healthier, healthiest)

2. In my opinion, watermelon is the _____ fruit in the world.
   (sweetier, sweeter, sweetest)

Activity 2

Add *-er* or *-est* to the underlined adjective to make each comparative or superlative.

> $Example:$ Davis purchased the <u>large</u> pumpkin at the farmers' market.
>
> large ⤳ largest
>
> Davis purchased the <u>largest</u> pumpkin at the farmers' market.

1. John's Fruit Stand is the <u>new</u> farmers' market in Missouri. _____

2. They have the <u>fresh</u> fruits and vegetables around. _____

3. John's tomatoes are <u>ripe</u> than the tomatoes in the supermarket. _____

4. His produce is also <u>cheap</u> than most other stores in the area. _____

5. John is also one of the <u>friendly</u> people I know. _____

CAPITALIZING TITLES

Capitalizing words within a title is a standard rule. In titles, most words are generally capitalized, including the first and last word, and every important word in between. There are also lowercase words in titles. These are usually the short words, or words fewer than five letters long, such as: *a, and, the, but, or, for, nor, on, at,* and *from*. However, pronouns and nouns that are less than five letters would still be capitalized: *You, My, Me, We, They, I,* and *Our*.

Cross out each uppercase letter that should not be capitalized in the titles below.
Circle each lowercase letter that should be capitalized.

1. Healthy Meals With Apples And Oranges

2. Delicious healthy recipes

3. The vitamins in My Food

4. Way Up High In The Apple Tree

Challenge: Write your own title about healthy food or healthy eating, using at least one comparative or superlative adjective in the title.

_____

_____

Get Up and Move!

1   Did you know that each time you exercise you are doing something wonderful for your body? Former First Lady Michelle Obama says that eating healthy food and staying physically active are the keys to a long and happy life. Many doctors suggest that kids should exercise for at least 60 minutes every day.

Overcoming the Challenge

2   There are many different ways that people exercise. Playing different sports, such as running, bowling, and swimming, can keep you moving. But how can you meet the challenge of getting daily exercise with a busy schedule?

3   Sometimes you can do this without even realizing it. Have you ever walked or ridden your bike to school instead of riding in a bus or a car? How about climbing the stairs instead of taking the elevator? Perhaps playing tag with a friend during recess? Walking, riding your bike, climbing stairs, and playing tag are forms of exercise that you can do every day.

Exercising the Body and Mind

4   Why is exercise important? Physical activity helps your bones, muscles, and joints grow and become strong. Bones and muscles work together to give you balance and coordination when you move. High-energy activities can make your heart strong. This will help blood and oxygen circulate better throughout your body. Being physically active helps to control weight. As a result, you will have less of a chance to develop problems such as Type 2 diabetes or heart disease. Additionally, studies show that children who exercise regularly feel good about themselves, sleep better, and are more ready to learn in school.

Beware of the Exercise Thief!

5   Look out! Many people spend too much time sitting down in one place. When a person spends more time surfing the Web, playing computer games, or watching television, the time left for exercising decreases. It is important to balance your time each day between activities that keep you moving along and ones that do not.

Types of Exercise

6   There are three important elements of exercise. These are *endurance*, *strength*, and *flexibility*. Taking part in a variety of activities can help you develop all three of these qualities. Endurance is the ability to exercise for a long period of time without getting tired, such as running from another child when playing tag at recess. Strength is the amount of power you may use when doing things like crossing the monkey bars. Flexibility refers to the complete range of motion in your joints and muscles. This affects how well you can bend over and move your body around. Sitting cross-legged without feeling pain or bending over to tie your shoes requires good flexibility.

7   Exercise is a great way to improve your health, feel better, and have fun. Whenever you possibly can, use every opportunity to get up and move!

Digging Deeper

Keep Your Bones Healthy!

There are so many ways to exercise! Think about the different activities that you can do. Make notes of some of your favorite ones to try with a friend or an adult.

UNDERSTANDING WORDS AND PHRASES

After reading the article "Get Up and Move!," complete the crossword puzzle using the word bank below.

word bank

- joints
- surfing the Web
- endurance
- strength
- flexibility
- disease
- bones
- exercise
- muscles

Across

3. an illness that prevents the body or mind from working normally
5. places where two bones meet in the body
6. searching the Internet
8. a physical activity to make one healthy or strong
9. hard pieces that form a person's or an animal's skeleton

Down

1. the quality of being physically strong
2. having this quality in muscles allows for more movement around the joints
4. the ability to do something difficult for a long time
7. body tissues that produce movement

DISTINGUISHING POINTS OF VIEW

After reading "Get Up and Move!," fill in the chart below to show the author's point of view. Afterward, fill in your own point of view.

Title: _____

Topic: _____

The author of the text believes:

_____

_____

The following are reasons why the author believes this:

_____

_____

_____

I believe:

_____

_____

My reasons for believing this are:

_____

_____

_____

HOW TO USE COMMAS

Commas have many uses. It is important to correctly use commas when you write an address. Commas separate the street address, city, state, and country.

Activity 1

Read the letter. Add commas to the letter as needed.

456 Little Street
Cojack MO 00987
August 8, 2024

Dear Travin,

I am having a great time at summer camp here in Venus Wyoming. We have been hiking, swimming, and playing volleyball and tennis. I never thought exercising could be so much fun. Tomorrow we are competing in a volleyball tournament in Summerton Wyoming.

When I return home, my family is taking us to Walt Disney World in Orlando Florida. It will be so much fun! Maybe you can come with us. The camp's address is 322 Woodland Drive Venus WY in case you would like to send me a letter.

Your friend,
Destiny

Activity 2

Answer the questions and rewrite the sentence using commas and/or quotation marks as needed.

1. In what city and state were you born?

   _____

2. What is your school's address?

   _____

Reading and Writing: Informational Texts

UNDERSTANDING ROOT WORDS

Identifying and knowing the meaning of Greek and Latin roots is important to understanding the meaning of unfamiliar words.

A root is a word part that can be added to other word parts to form words with common meanings. For example, the Greek word root **bio** means "life." **Bio** can be added to other word parts to make new words.

> Example: **Bio** + **logy** = biology. The study of living things.
>
> **Bio** + **graphy** = biography. A written account of someone else's life.

Activity 1

The Greek root *scope* means "to see, look, or examine." Draw a line from each word to its definition. Then, write a sentence using each word in the space below.

Word	Meaning	Your Sentence
telescope	a tube that has mirrors and loose pieces of colored glass or plastic inside at one end so that you see many different patterns when you turn the tube while looking in through the other end	
microscope	an instrument that is used for listening to someone's heart or lungs	
kaleidoscope	a device shaped like a long tube that you look through in order to see things that are far away	
stethoscope	a tool used for producing a much larger view of very small objects so that they can be seen clearly	

Activity 2

On the basketball hoop below, look at the root word, its origin, and its meaning. Then, list four words that use the root, along with their definitions on each of the basketballs below.

Root: Phone
Origin: Greek
Meaning: Sound

WRITE YOUR OPINION

In the article "Get Up and Move!," doctors suggest that kids should exercise for at least 60 minutes each day. Do you agree or disagree with this statement?

Write an opinion essay stating your answer. Be sure your essay has a topic sentence (or main idea) that tells your opinion. Next, list three reasons why you believe, or do not believe, that kids should exercise for 60 minutes each day. Finally, write a conclusion that restates your opinion. Use the graphic organizer below to help you plan your essay.

Topic sentence: _____

_____

_____

Reason 1: _____

_____

_____

Reason 2: _____

_____

_____

Reason 3: _____

_____

_____

Conclusion: _____

_____

_____

_____

REVIEW

Congratulations! You have completed the units in this section. Now you will have the chance to practice some of the skills you just learned.

Reading Fluency

Adults: Time your student reading aloud for one minute. Make a note of where your student is at the end of one minute. (Your student should be able to read between 90 and 110 words per minute.) Have your student continue reading to the end of the passage to answer the questions that follow.

Butterfly Travels

Yesterday, Mom and I watched a video about butterflies. I learned how easy it is for me to	18
have a garden full of butterflies. Mom and I made a plan to go to the store the next day to	39
buy the plants we needed. We talked with the man at the store and found out milkweed is	57
the best attractor of butterflies. We went home with five plants to put in our yard.	73
By the end of the summer, we had so many butterflies around our yard that I would	90
see them floating by when I walked outside. The man at the store told us to put netting	108
around a plant in order for a caterpillar to attach to it. Then we could watch it change into	127
a chrysalis. It worked! Mom and I did a little more research to figure out how long they	145
take to emerge, or hatch. We found out they usually take 10 to 14 days. That meant ours	163
were almost ready.	166
Finally, our butterflies started coming out. The butterflies were all hanging upside-	178
down by their feet. They were opening and closing their wings so slowly. Mom told me	194
this is how they dry them to be ready to fly. After two days, our butterflies were ready to	213
go free. Mom and I took off the netting and watched the butterflies take their first flight.	230

Words read in 1 minute – errors = WPM

After reading "Butterfly Travels," answer the language review questions below.

Activity 1

Capitalize these titles:

1. marley the magnificent butterfly

2. from caterpillar to butterfly

3. a world of butterflies

4. My, oh my—a butterfly

Activity 2

Revise the following simple, compound, and complex sentences.

1. I like to catch butterflies with my friends. I like to watch butterflies with my friends.
   (Change from simple to compound)

   _____

2. The students are studying about chrysalises because they have a test tomorrow.
   (Change from complex to simple)

   _____

3. I tried to teach my friend about caterpillars, and my friend tried to teach me about ladybugs.
   (Change from compound to complex)

   _____

Activity 3

Use what you learned about suffixes to determine the meanings of new words.

1. Add the suffix -*ship* (the state or quality of) to the word *friend*. **Friendship** means:

   _____

2. Add the suffix -*ment* (the action of) to the word *excite*. **Excitement** means:

   _____

3. Add the suffix -*ful* (full of) to the word *color*. **Colorful** means:

   _____

The following is a student's journal entry about an important nutrition lesson.

April 24, 2023

Dear Diary,

Last month, my class had guest speaker, Miss Allison, talk about nutrition using the MyPlate program. Miss Allison explained how eating good amounts of fruits and vegetables helps keep our bodies healthy. I learned that vegetables should take up the largest section on my plate. She also stated that there are a variety of vegetables to choose from: dark green, starchy, red and orange, beans, and peas. After Miss Allison left, I wondered, "How many servings of vegetables should I eat each day?"

I asked my dad to help me find the answer to this question. Dad found a website on the computer that shows MyPlate. The plate is split up by how much of each kind of item you should eat each day. We read a chart that said that girls my age should eat 1½ cups of vegetables every day, while boys the same age need 2 cups. This gave me a great idea!

"Let's grow a vegetable garden," I said to Dad. Together, Dad and I got the supplies to begin planting. I read on my tablet that vegetables need a place in the ground that gets six to eight hours of full sun. Once Dad and I found the perfect spot, we began putting down fresh soil. Next, we dug holes deep enough for the plant sprouts. Finally, we gave the plants some water. Dad told me, "It's important to water them every day so they don't die."

Soon, I began to see vegetables growing from these plants. I checked them every day for bugs or other animal bites. When the vegetables were finally ripe enough to pick, Dad and I picked them together. We were careful to pull from the tip touching the plant so the stem would not break. We couldn't wait to use the vegetables for dinner!

I was so excited about my experience that I asked my teacher if I could write a note to Miss Allison. In my letter, I made sure to thank her for teaching my class about being healthy. Then, I told Miss Allison all about our vegetable garden. I even drew a picture in the letter for her. At the end of the letter, I signed it: Natasha (the vegetable grower).

After reading the journal entry, answer the questions below.

1. Reread paragraph 3 of the journal entry. Step by step, list the four necessary things you must do in order to grow a vegetable garden.

_____

_____

_____

_____

2. What was the result of Natasha's efforts?

_____

_____

3. Is Natasha relating information or is she trying to convince you of an idea?

_____

_____

4. Do you think it is important to grow your own vegetables or buy them from the store? Why do you feel this way?

_____

_____

5. Look at the illustration of the food plate. How does this picture relate to the journal entry?

_____

_____

6. What information can you obtain from the picture of MyPlate that you can apply in your own life?

_____

_____

_____

DISCOVER

Write Your Opinion

Writing an opinion essay allows you to express your own point of view. An opinion is a belief or feeling that must be supported by reasons.

Your school is thinking about planting a community garden. Do you think this is a good idea? Why or why not? Write an opinion essay explaining the benefits or disadvantages of the community garden. Use the graphic organizer below.

State your opinion. (Yes or no to a school community garden?)

_____

_____

_____

_____

Describe in detail how this would change things.

_____

_____

_____

_____

Describe the benefits of your suggestion. (Why should this change be made or not be made?)

_____

_____

_____

_____

Write Your Essay

Use your outline from page 68 to develop your essay below.

Introduction (Opinion sentence):

_____

_____

_____

_____

Body (Describe the change and the benefits):

_____

_____

_____

_____

_____

_____

_____

_____

_____

_____

Conclusion (Restate your opinion):

_____

_____

_____

_____

Remember to use your *My Journal* pages at the back of the workbook if you need more space to write.

Reading and Writing: Literature

Author Study: Adventures in Fantasy

In this section, you will read stories, myths, and poems with amazing plots, interesting characters, and beautiful word pictures.

Reading literature provides a look into an author's thoughts and feelings. It also reflects our world and the different ways that people behave. Even though the material in this section is fictional, valuable life lessons can be learned. Reading literature can affect how you think and feel, which in turn can shape your actions.

Writing about literature will cause you to organize your thoughts so that you will be able to clearly state your point of view. As you write, new discoveries in your thinking will create connections to ideas and concepts that you already know. Working through what at first may seem challenging will open new pathways of learning, understanding, and communicating.

While reading literature teaches you how other people behave, writing about literature teaches you about yourself!

Happy reading and writing!

AUTHOR STUDY: ADVENTURES IN FANTASY

This unit covers two adventure and fantasy stories by Lewis Carroll: *Alice's Adventures in Wonderland* and *Through the Looking-Glass*.

You will be able to evaluate the themes and characters and make connections between the stories in this two-part lesson.

Let's first read about the author Lewis Carroll.

Lewis Carroll was born in 1832. His writing career began early when he wrote poems for his own homemade newspaper. As a student, he did very well in writing and math. Later, he became a photographer until 1881. That year, he decided to spend all of his time writing stories. While Carroll is well known for his many poems and books, he is best remembered for his "Alice" stories, which are still popular today!

Later, you're going to read a short excerpt of Lewis Carroll's work. Remember to think about how the characters and lessons are alike.

Let's begin!

Alice is a young girl who fell down a rabbit hole and found herself in Wonderland. Here, she is at a tea party with the Hatter and his friends.

Alice's Adventures in Wonderland

by Lewis Carroll

Excerpt from the chapter "A Mad Tea-Party"

"What a funny watch!" she remarked. "It tells the day of the month, and doesn't tell what o'clock it is!"

"Have you guessed the riddle yet?" the Hatter said, turning to Alice again.

"No, I give up," Alice replied: "What's the answer?"

"I haven't the slightest idea," said the Hatter.

"Nor I," said the March Hare.

Alice sighed **wearily**. "I think you might do something better with the time," she said "than wasting it asking riddles with no answers."

"If you knew Time as well as I do," said the Hatter, "you wouldn't talk about wasting *it*. It's *him*."

"I don't know what you mean," said Alice.

"Of course you don't!" the Hatter said, **tossing** his head **contemptuously**. "I daresay you never spoke to Time!"

"Perhaps not," Alice **cautiously** replied. "But I know I have to beat time when I learn music."

"Ah! that accounts for it," said the Hatter. "He won't stand beating. Now, if you only kept on good terms with him, he'd do almost anything you liked with the clock. For instance, suppose it were nine o'clock in the morning, just time to begin lessons: you'd only have to whisper a hint to Time, and round goes the clock in a twinkling! Half-past one, time for dinner!"

("I only wish it was," the March Hare said to itself in a whisper.)

"That would be grand, certainly," said Alice thoughtfully: "but then—I shouldn't be hungry for it, you know."

"Not at first, perhaps," said the Hatter: "but you could keep it to half-past one as long as you liked."

"Is that the way *you* manage?" Alice asked.

The Hatter shook his head **mournfully**. "Not I!" he replied.

glossary

cautiously: Acting carefully

contemptuously: Acting with disgust or hate

mournfully: Full of sadness

wearily: Without much strength or energy

DESCRIBING CHARACTERS

Remember, sometimes stories by the same author have characters that are alike. Keep this in mind when you read the second story in Lesson Two.

Read the excerpt from *Alice's Adventures in Wonderland*. Circle the best answer for the questions below.

1. Which word **best** describes Alice?
   A. shy
   B. silly
   C. curious
   D. bored

2. How does Alice feel when she finds there is no answer to the riddle?
   A. bothered
   B. cheerful
   C. nervous
   D. afraid

PICTURES HELP WITH UNDERSTANDING

1. In the picture below, what type of face is Alice making? Is she enjoying the tea party? Why or why not?

_____

_____

_____

_____

_____

_____

2. What mood, or feelings, does the picture create?

_____

_____

_____

_____

_____

_____

3. What if the picture showed Alice smiling at the table? How would that change the mood being created by the picture?

_____

_____

_____

_____

_____

_____

_____

_____

_____

Remember to use your *My Journal* pages at the back of the workbook if you need more space to write.

LANGUAGE—THE EFFECT OF WORDS AND SHADES OF MEANING

If you want to color a picture of a bright blue ocean on a sunny day, you may open up your box of crayons and find that there are six shades of blue to choose from. It is important that you select the right shade of blue. Just like choosing the right blue color for the right picture is important, knowing exactly what a word means will help you choose the right one for what you want to say. There are some words that seem to have the same meaning as other words. However, when you look at each of these words more closely, their different definitions can change the entire meaning of a sentence.

Example: Read this sentence from the story.

"If you knew Time as well as I do," said the Hatter, "you wouldn't talk about wasting it. It's *him*."

The word **knew** is very certain. In other words, there are no ifs, ands, or maybes. When the Hatter says, "If you *knew* Time as well as I do," he is making it clear to Alice that he can tell her everything there is to know about Time.

Read this sentence from the story.

"Of course you don't!" the Hatter said, **tossing** *his head contemptuously. "I daresay you never spoke to Time!"*

Answer the following questions.

1. What image does **tossing** make you think of?

    _____

    _____

    _____

    _____

    _____

2. What if **shaking** or **moving** were used instead of **tossing**? Would the image you have of the Hatter be different? Why or why not?

_____

_____

_____

_____

_____

_____

Challenge: Read the list of words below and match each word to its similar meaning. Then think about how that would change the meaning of the example sentence on page 78 if one of these words were used instead of "knew."

1. believed

2. suspected

3. heard

4. wondered

a. was told that something was true

b. imagined that something might be true

c. felt for sure that something was true

d. had an idea that something was probably true

NARRATIVE WRITING

A **narrative** is a written story that tells you about real or imagined experiences. To write a good narrative story, remember to include dialogue, descriptive language, and your five senses (sight, smell, taste, touch, and hearing) to describe things that tell the story in an organized sequence.

Have you ever had dinner at someone else's home for a special occasion or holiday? Use that experience to write your story. If you do not have a real-life story, then you can make one up for this assignment.

Ask yourself these questions before you start writing: Who was at the dinner? Did you know the guests? What type of food was served? Was it a new type of food for you? Was the table decorated in a special way? Did you have to wear special clothes?

Use your five senses to write your story. What do you smell? What does the food taste like? What color are the decorations? Should there be music playing? Also, remember to use dialogue. What do the characters say to each other? The reader should be able to imagine the action in the story and understand the characters' thoughts and feelings from what you write. In your conclusion, discuss how everyone felt at the end of the special meal.

Introduction (Set up your story. Who is in it? Where and when is it set?):

_____

_____

_____

_____

Event 1 (What happened first in your story? Use sensory details):

_____

_____

_____

_____

_____

Event 2 (Then what happened? Use sensory details):

_____

_____

_____

_____

Event 3 (What happened last? Use sensory details):

_____

_____

_____

_____

Conclusion (Did you enjoy the meal and the people at the table? Why or why not?):

_____

_____

_____

_____

Alice slips through a looking glass, or mirror, and finds herself on another adventure in a strange land. Here she meets Humpty Dumpty.

Through the Looking-Glass

by Lewis Carroll

Excerpt from the chapter "Humpty Dumpty"

Humpty Dumpty took the book, and looked at it carefully. "That seems to be done right—" he began.

"You're holding it upside down!" Alice interrupted.

"To be sure I was!" Humpty Dumpty said gaily, as she turned it round for him. "I thought it looked a little queer. As I was saying, that SEEMS to be done right—though I haven't time to look it over thoroughly just now—and that shows that there are three hundred and sixty-four days when you might get un-birthday presents—"

"Certainly," said Alice.

"And only ONE for birthday presents, you know. There's glory for you!"

"I don't know what you mean by 'glory,'" Alice said.

Humpty Dumpty smiled contemptuously. "Of course you don't—till I tell you. I meant 'there's a nice knock-down argument for you!'"

"But 'glory' doesn't mean 'a nice knock-down argument,'" Alice objected.

"When *I* use a word," Humpty Dumpty said in rather a **scornful** tone, "it means just what I choose it to mean—neither more nor less."

"The question is," said Alice, "whether you CAN make words mean so many different things."

"The question is," said Humpty Dumpty, "which is to be master—that's all."

Alice was too much **puzzled** to say anything, so after a minute Humpty Dumpty began again. "They've a temper, some of them—particularly verbs, they're the proudest—adjectives you can do anything with, but not verbs—however, *I* can manage the whole lot of them! **Impenetrability**! That's what I say!"

"Would you tell me, please," said Alice, "what that means?"

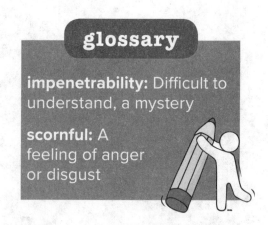

glossary

impenetrability: Difficult to understand, a mystery

scornful: A feeling of anger or disgust

"Now you talk like a reasonable child," said Humpty Dumpty, looking very much pleased. "I meant by 'impenetrability' that we've had enough of that subject, and it would be just as well if you'd mention what you mean to do next, as I suppose you don't mean to stop here all the rest of your life."

"That's a great deal to make one word mean," Alice said in a thoughtful tone.

"When I make a word do a lot of work like that," said Humpty Dumpty, "I always pay it extra."

"Oh!" said Alice. She was too much puzzled to make any other remark.

"Ah, you should see 'em come round me of a Saturday night," Humpty Dumpty went on, wagging his head gravely from side to side: "for to get their wages, you know."

(Alice didn't venture to ask what he paid them with; and so you see I can't tell YOU.)

UNDERSTANDING THE STORY

After reading the "Humpty Dumpty" excerpt from *Through the Looking-Glass*, answer the questions below.

1. What is the **main** problem that Alice and Humpty Dumpty are discussing?

   A. a "knock-down" argument

   B. the meaning of words

   C. an "un-birthday" present

   D. the number of days in a year

2. Who gets paid for working extra?

   A. Alice

   B. Humpty Dumpty

   C. days

   D. words

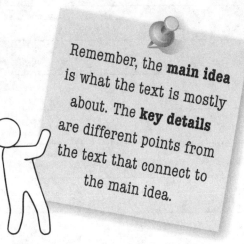

Remember, the **main idea** is what the text is mostly about. The **key details** are different points from the text that connect to the main idea.

Reading and Writing: Literature

COMPARING AND CONTRASTING STORIES BY THE SAME AUTHOR

1. After reading the excerpts from *Alice's Adventures in Wonderland* and from *Through the Looking-Glass*, describe how the stories are similar on the lines below.

_____

_____

_____

_____

_____

_____

_____

_____

2. Both of these stories are called fantasies because events within the stories do not happen in real life. What are the different events that happen in each story that could never really happen? Fill in the chart below.

Alices's Adventures in Wonderland	Through the Looking-Glass
_____	_____
_____	_____
_____	_____
_____	_____
_____	_____

UNDERSTANDING POSSESSIVES

When a noun is made into a possessive, it shows ownership. This occurs by adding an *apostrophe* and an *s* ('s) to the end of the word. If it is already plural (more than one), you simply put an apostrophe after the last *s*.

> **Example:** The imagination of the girl ⟶ The girl's imagination
>
> The school of the students ⟶ The students' school

1. In the following sentences, place the apostrophe in the correct place.

   A. Un-birthday presents added up to a years worth of days minus one.

   B. The books pages were hard to read upside down.

   C. Verbs behaved badly compared to adjectives actions.

   D. The "Alice" stories popularity has lasted for over 150 years.

2. In the following sentences, fill in the blank with the correct possessive noun.

   A. Most of the answers to _____ questions made no sense.

   B. _____ book was upside down until Alice turned it right side up.

   C. Humpty Dumpty changed a _____ meaning whenever he wanted.

   D. _____ two most famous books were about Alice.

USING REFERENCE MATERIAL

Read the dictionary entry:

puzzled (pə-zəld) verb 1. to not understand

Now read this sentence from *Through the Looking-Glass*:

"*Alice was too much **puzzled** to say anything, so after a minute Humpty Dumpty began again.*"

Which word could you use instead of **puzzled** to create the same mood in the sentence from the story?

   A. surprised   C. amused

   B. confused   D. saddened

WRITE YOUR ADVENTURE STORY

Adventure and fantasy stories are great fun to write because your imagination can go wild! The setting can be anywhere you want—real or imaginary. Animals, plants, and all kinds of other objects can talk and interact with each other. Time and space can be presented wherever and however you wish. Nevertheless, even in adventure and fantasy writing, the story still needs to make sense to the reader.

Write an adventure story that describes events that lead up to an exciting moment. Think about where you want to set the story and what characters you will choose. What can happen in your story that can't happen in real life? Use any of your five senses (sight, smell, touch, taste, and hearing) to describe everyone and everything in the story, so readers can feel like they are there.

Adventure and fantasy story: _____

Setting: _____

Time period: _____

Characters: _____

Exciting moment: _____

Introduction (Set up your story):

_____

_____

_____

Event 1 (What first happened in your story? Use sensory details):

_____

_____

_____

_____

Event 2 (Then what happened? Use sensory details):

_____

_____

_____

_____

Event 3 (What finally happened? Use sensory details):

_____

_____

_____

_____

Conclusion (Describe the exciting moment):

_____

_____

_____

_____

Books by the Same Author

In this unit, you will read excerpts of stories from the author Frances Hodgson Burnett.

Let's first learn about this author.

Frances Hodgson Burnett was born in England in 1849. She was from a poor family and often wrote stories to escape from the daily struggles they faced. In 1865, her family moved to America. Frances used her talent to earn money by writing short stories for different American magazines. She married Dr. Swan Burnett in 1873. In her career, she wrote over forty books and became a world-famous children's story author.

As you read on, you may want to keep a journal. You can record facts about the passages, characters, plots, and settings, as well as your own thoughts about what you read. Use this information to help answer the questions and to complete the writing activities.

Happy reading and writing!

This fountain in Central Park, New York City, honors children's book author Frances Hodgson Burnett, who wrote *The Secret Garden*.

Sara is a new student at a school for girls. Lavinia does not like her and has been waiting for a chance to embarrass her in front of her classmates.

A Little Princess

by Frances Hodgson Burnett
Excerpt from Chapter 6, "The Diamond Mines"

1   Here was Lavinia's opportunity.

"Ah, yes, your royal highness," she said. "We are princesses, I believe. At least one of us is. The school ought to be very fashionable now Miss Minchin has a princess for a pupil."

2   Sara started toward her. She looked as if she were going to box her ears. Perhaps she was. Her trick of pretending things was the joy of her life. She never spoke of it to girls she was not fond of. Her new "pretend" about being a princess was very near to her heart, and she was shy and sensitive about it. She had meant it to be rather a secret, and here was Lavinia **deriding** it before nearly all the school. She felt the blood rush up into her face and tingle in her ears. She only just saved herself. If you were a princess, you did not fly into rages. Her hand dropped, and she stood quite still a moment. When she spoke, it was in a quiet, steady voice; she held her head up, and everybody listened to her.

3   "It's true," she said. "Sometimes I do pretend I am a princess. I pretend I am a princess, so that I can try and behave like one."

4   Lavinia could not think of exactly the right thing to say. Several times she had found that she could not think of a satisfactory reply when she was dealing with Sara. The reason for this was that, somehow, the rest always seemed to be **vaguely** in **sympathy** with her opponent. She saw now that they were pricking up their ears interestedly. The truth was, they liked princesses, and they all hoped they might hear something more definite about this one, and drew nearer Sara accordingly.

glossary

deriding: To talk about something in a mean way

sympathy: To be sorry for someone else's troubles

vaguely: Not clearly expressed

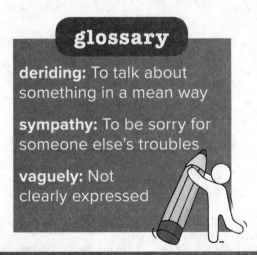

UNDERSTANDING THE STORY

After reading the excerpt from *A Little Princess*, answer the questions below.

1. What was Sara's secret?

    A. She pretended to be a princess.

    B. She did not like the other girls.

    C. She did not know the rights things to say.

    D. She could control her temper at all times.

2. What did the girls do at the end of the passage?

    A. They acted like princesses for Miss Minchin.

    B. They talked in low, steady voices.

    C. They moved closer to Sara.

    D. They dressed up like princesses.

3. Which two sentences describe the setting of the story?

    _____

    _____

DESCRIBING CHARACTERS

1. How do Lavinia's actions help move the plot along?

    A. She causes the other girls to hate Sara.

    B. She becomes Sara's best friend.

    C. She gets Sara to admit her secret.

    D. She makes Sara cry in front of everyone.

2. How do princesses behave, in Sara's mind?

    A. They lose their temper.

    B. They control their temper.

    C. They look down on people.

    D. They admire other people.

UNDERSTANDING THE PARTS OF A STORY

Read the excerpt from *A Little Princess* again, then answer the following questions.

1. How does the first paragraph affect the rest of the story? How different would the story be if it began with the third paragraph instead?

   _____

   _____

   _____

   _____

   _____

   _____

2. How does the fourth paragraph move the story along? How would the story change if this paragraph were left out?

   _____

   _____

   _____

   _____

   _____

   _____

3. Would the story be different if the last paragraph became the first paragraph? Explain.

   _____

   _____

   _____

   _____

   _____

UNDERSTANDING DIFFERENT POINTS OF VIEW

Activity 1

Read this sentence from the story.

"When she spoke it was in a quiet, steady voice; she held her head up, and everybody listened to her."

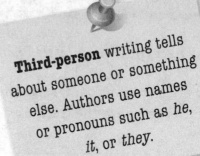

Third-person writing tells about someone or something else. Authors use names or pronouns such as *he, it,* or *they.*

1. Is this sentence written in third person? How do you know? Circle the words or phrases in the sentence that give you clues to your answer.

2. Pretend you are Sara. Now, write the same sentence, but in first person.

Activity 2

What do you imagine Sara is thinking and feeling while she is talking about her secret to the other girls? Put yourself in Sara's shoes. Think about the feelings you may have talking about a secret in front of your classmates.

List these thoughts and feelings in the chart below for both Sara and you. Which are different? Which are the same?

Sara's Feelings and Thoughts	Your Feelings and Thoughts

CONNECTING WORDS

A **conjunction** is a part of speech that joins or connects parts of a sentence. There are two types of conjunctions: simple and subordinating.

Simple conjunctions always come *between* the words or clauses that they join. An easy way to remember some common simple conjunctions is by repeating the word FANBOYS.

FANBOYS: For-And-Nor-But-Or-Yet-So

> ## Example:
>
> Sara likes [tea] **and** [coffee].
>
> The simple conjunction *and* comes between the words that it is joining together (tea and coffee).
>
> [Sara likes to pretend], **but** [her imagination sometimes gets her in trouble].
>
> The simple conjunction *but* joins two clauses that could be complete sentences on their own. When this happens, it is always correct to place a comma right before the conjunction.

Subordinating conjunctions come at the *beginning* of a group of related words that have a subject and verb but cannot stand on their own.

> ## Example:
>
> **Because** Sara was shy, she did not want to give a speech.
>
> Other common subordinating conjunctions are *after, although, unless, while, before, if,* and *once.*

CONNECTING WORDS

Activity 1

Read the following sentences and place a simple conjunction in the blank to make the sentence make sense. Use the following word bank.

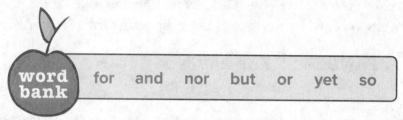

word bank   for   and   nor   but   or   yet   so

Fill in the blank with the simple conjunction that best fits each sentence.

1. Lavinia saw a chance to embarrass Sara, _____ she made fun of her wanting to be a princess.

2. Sara raised her hand to Lavinia, _____ she stopped herself in time.

3. The girls were very quiet, _____ they wanted to listen to Sara and Lavinia.

4. Sara had a secret, _____ she wanted to keep it to herself.

Activity 2

Use the subordinating conjunction word bank to fill in the blanks of the next two sentences.

1. _____ Lavinia did not understand Sara, she did not know how to answer her.

    A. After   C. Because
    B. Than   D. If only

2. The girls would have behaved better _____ Miss Minchin had been in the room.

    A. if   C. even though
    B. where   D. that

word bank

after
although
as
as if
as long as
as though
because
before
even if
even though
if
if only
once
since
so that
than

Mary is an orphan who is sent to her uncle's house to live in England. Her cousin, Colin, is very sick and has to stay in bed. When Mary finds a walled-up garden on her uncle's land, she wants to tell Colin all about it.

The Secret Garden

by Frances Hodgson Burnett
Excerpt from Chapter 13, "I Am Colin"

[Colin] leaned still farther forward.

"A secret," he said. "What do you mean? Tell me."

Mary's words almost tumbled over one another.

"You see—you see," she panted, "if no one knows but ourselves—if there was a door, hidden somewhere under the ivy—if there was—and we could find it; and if we could slip through it together and shut it behind us, and no one knew any one was inside and we called it our garden and pretended that—that we were **missel thrushes** and it was our nest, and if we played there almost every day and dug and planted seeds and made it all come alive—"

"Is it dead?" he interrupted her.

"It soon will be if no one cares for it," she went on. "The bulbs will live but the roses—" He stopped her again as excited as she was herself.

"What are bulbs?" he put in quickly.

"They are daffodils and lilies and snowdrops. They are working in the earth now—pushing up pale green points because the spring is coming."

"Is the spring coming?" he said. "What is it like? You don't see it in rooms if you are ill."

"It is the sun shining on the rain and the rain falling on the sunshine, and things pushing up and working under the earth," said Mary. "If the garden was a secret and we could get into it we could watch the things grow bigger every day, and see how many roses are alive. Don't you see? Oh, don't you see how much nicer it would be if it was a secret?"

He dropped back on his pillow and lay there with an odd expression on his face.

Digging Deeper

Plant Your Own Garden!

You don't need a secret garden to learn how to plant flowers and vegetables. What types of flowers and plants would you grow in a garden? Kids Gardening and the National Gardening Association have teamed up to help kids plan and start gardens of their own.

UNDERSTANDING THE STORY

After reading the excerpt from *A Secret Garden*, answer the following questions.

1. Number the different things that happened within the story in the correct order.

    _____ Colin falls back on his pillow.

    _____ Mary talks about what happens in spring.

    _____ Colin asks what Mary means by a secret.

    _____ Mary says they can find the door to the garden.

2. What type of animal is a **missel thrush**? What clue in the story supports your answer? Explain.

    _____

    _____

    _____

    _____

3. Colin asks Mary if spring was coming. He is sick in his room and may not be able to see it, so he wants to know what this will be like. How does Mary describe the coming of spring?

    _____

    _____

    _____

    _____

    _____

    _____

    _____

    _____

DESCRIBING CHARACTERS

After reading the excerpt from *A Secret Garden*, circle the best answer for the questions below.

1. Why is Mary telling Colin the secret?

   A. so he can pick roses in the spring with her

   B. so he can learn all about flowers with her

   C. so he can play and plant seeds with her

   D. so he can push up the pale green points with her

2. How does Colin feel about the secret?

   A. angry

   B. interested

   C. puzzled

   D. afraid

Reading and Writing: Literature

COMPARING AND CONTRASTING STORIES BY THE SAME AUTHOR

1. After reading the excerpts from *A Little Princess* and *The Secret Garden*, describe how the stories are similar. Fill in the lines below.

_____

_____

_____

_____

_____

_____

_____

_____

2. After reading the excerpts from *A Little Princess* and *The Secret Garden*, describe how the stories are different. Fill in the chart below.

A Little Princess	The Secret Garden

CHANGING WORD ENDINGS

There are words that we use all the time when we speak or write. These words are called *high-frequency* words. Many high-frequency words—mostly nouns, adjectives, and verbs—can have their meaning changed by adding a suffix to the base words. Some high-frequency words are spelled very differently when they change their role in a sentence, especially verbs.

Some words can be made plural by just adding an "s" or "es," but other words can be more stubborn. A simple "s" will not do! You can change many words that end in "y" by following a few easy rules.

> **Example:** Think of this rule like a simple math problem: subtract "y" from the base word, and then add "i." Then add an "es" after the "i" to get your new form of the word.
>
> For example, see how the word in the parentheses changes from singular to plural to fill in the blank.
>
> Roses and daffodils come from different flower _____ (family).
>
> family − y = fam + il
>
> = fam + il + i + es = families

Change the word in the parentheses to plural and finish the sentence.

1. A garden of flowers usually will attract _____ (butterfly).

2. Mary and Colin would not see as many gardens in _____ (city).

3. We went to the botanical gardens and saw a lovely field of _____ (pansy).

Reading and Writing: Literature

LEARNING ABOUT WORD FAMILIES

Words can also be placed into different types of groups. Sometimes they are grouped by how they are spelled, what letter combinations they use, what sounds they make, or what rules they follow.

> *Example:* Read the sentence:
>
> "They are daffodils and lilies and snowdrops. They are working in the earth now—pushing up pale green points because the *spring* is coming."
>
> The word **spring** has many members in its word family because of its *–ing* sound. Look at the following words that end in *–ing*:
>
> | | | |
> |---|---|---|
> | bring | sing | thing |
> | king | string | wing |

List three words that belong in the same family for each word in the chart.

Day

1. _____
2. _____
3. _____

Nest

1. _____
2. _____
3. _____

Slip

1. _____
2. _____
3. _____

WRITE YOUR EXPLANATION

Can you keep a secret? Think about planning a surprise for a friend or someone in your family. Should you keep it a secret, or should you tell someone else? Maybe another person could help you plan the surprise. That person, however, could also spoil the surprise by telling the wrong person. What do you think?

After reading the excerpt from *The Secret Garden* on page 95, use the organizer to plan a five-paragraph essay. In your essay, write about how sharing secrets with friends or family members can be either a good or bad idea. Let's begin!

Introduction (Topic sentence stating the main idea):

_____

_____

_____

_____

_____

_____

_____

Event 1 (Supporting detail):

_____

_____

_____

_____

_____

_____

_____

Remember to use your *My Journal* pages at the back of the workbook if you need more space to write.

Event 2 (Supporting detail):

_____

_____

_____

_____

_____

Event 3 (Supporting detail):

_____

_____

_____

_____

_____

Conclusion (Concluding sentences that summarize the main idea):

_____

_____

_____

_____

_____

REVIEW

Reading Fluency

Adults: Time your student reading aloud for one minute. Make a note of where your student is at the end of one minute. (Your student should be able to read between 90 and 110 words per minute.) Have your student continue reading to the end of the passage.

Excerpt from

The Wind in the Willows

By Kenneth Grahame

"Now, the VERY next time this happens," said a gruff and suspicious voice, "I shall be	16
exceedingly angry. Who is it THIS time, disturbing people on such a night? Speak up!"	31
"Oh, Badger," cried the Rat, "let us in, please. It's me, Rat, and my friend Mole, and	48
we've lost our way in the snow."	55
"Why, Ratty, my dear little man!" exclaimed the Badger, in quite a different voice. "Come	70
along in, both of you, at once. Why, you must be perished. Well, I never! Lost in the snow!	89
And in the Wild Wood, too, and at this time of night! But come in with you."	106
The two animals tumbled over each other in their eagerness to get inside, and heard	121
the door shut behind them with great joy and relief.	131
The Badger, who wore a long dressing-gown, and whose slippers were indeed very down	145
at heel, carried a flat candlestick in his paw and had probably been on his way to bed when	164
their summons sounded. He looked kindly down on them and patted both their heads.	178
"This is not the sort of night for small animals to be out," he said paternally. "I'm afraid	196
you've been up to some of your pranks again, Ratty. But come along; come into the kitchen.	213
There's a first-rate fire there, and supper and everything."	222

Words read in 1 minute – errors = WPM

Activity 1

Select two conjunctions from the word bank. Then write two sentences using the conjunctions.

1. _____

2. _____

Activity 2

Write two sentences below, making sure to include possessive nouns.

1. _____

2. _____

word bank

although

as long as

even though

since

so

that

though

until

while

Activity 3

Review these suffix rules:

- Keep the final "e" if the suffix begins with a consonant.
- Double the final consonant if the word has one syllable or the suffix begins with a vowel.
- For a word ending in "y," drop the "y" and make it an "i."

1. Remove the suffix –*ness* from *happiness* _____

2. Add the suffix –*ed* to the word *skip* _____

3. Add the suffix –*es* to the word *cry* _____

Now look at these suffixes and their meanings. Write at least one word with each suffix. Then write a sentence with that word.

4. –*ist*: one who is an expert in _____

_____

5. –*ness*: state of being _____

_____

UNDERSTAND

Now, let's review and practice the reading skills that you learned in Units 5 and 6.

Excerpt from

The Wonderful Wizard of Oz

By L. Frank Baum

"What makes you a coward?" asked Dorothy, looking at the great beast in wonder, for he was as big as a small horse.

"It's a mystery," replied the Lion. "I suppose I was born that way. All the other animals in the forest naturally expect me to be brave, for the Lion is everywhere thought to be the King of Beasts. I learned that if I roared very loudly every living thing was frightened and got out of my way. Whenever I've met a man I've been awfully scared; but I just roared at him, and he has always run away as fast as he could go. If the elephants and the tigers and the bears had ever tried to fight me, I should have run myself—I'm such a coward; but just as soon as they hear me roar they all try to get away from me, and of course I let them go."

"But that isn't right. The King of Beasts shouldn't be a coward," said the Scarecrow.

"I know it," returned the Lion, wiping a tear from his eye with the tip of his tail. "It is my great sorrow, and makes my life very unhappy. But whenever there is danger, my heart begins to beat fast."

"Perhaps you have heart disease," said the Tin Woodman.

"It may be," said the Lion.

"If you have," continued the Tin Woodman, "you ought to be glad, for it proves you have a heart. For my part, I have no heart; so I cannot have heart disease."

"Perhaps," said the Lion thoughtfully, "if I had no heart I should not be a coward."

"Have you brains?" asked the Scarecrow.

"I suppose so. I've never looked to see," replied the Lion.

"I am going to the Great Oz to ask him to give me some," remarked the Scarecrow, "for my head is stuffed with straw."

"And I am going to ask him to give me a heart," said the Woodman.

"And I am going to ask him to send Toto and me back to Kansas," added Dorothy.

"Do you think Oz could give me courage?" asked the Cowardly Lion.

"Just as easily as he could give me brains," said the Scarecrow.

"Or give me a heart," said the Tin Woodman.

"Or send me back to Kansas," said Dorothy.

"Then, if you don't mind, I'll go with you," said the Lion, "for my life is simply unbearable without a bit of courage."

After reading the excerpt from *The Wizard of Oz*, answer the questions below.

1. Describe the Lion's problem in the story.

    _____

    _____

    _____

2. What motivates the Lion to find a resolution to his problem?

    _____

    _____

    _____

3. How do the Lion's actions affect the plot?

    _____

    _____

    _____

4. How does the second paragraph affect the rest of the story? In other words, if paragraph 2 were not included, how would the story be changed?

    _____

    _____

    _____

5. Imagine if the Scarecrow and Dorothy were missing from the story. Explain how this would change the story.

    _____

    _____

    _____

6. What word **best** describes how the Lion behaves throughout the story?

    _____

DISCOVER

Explanatory Writing

In Units 5 and 6, you read stories by the same author, as well as fantasy stories. You will use this information for your next exciting assignment!

Imagine that you are a story reviewer. People depend on what you say to help them make decisions about what to read. You will write an essay explaining why readers should either (1) read the work of a particular author who has written multiple stories, or (2) read a series of adventure fantasy stories.

With the help of an adult, discuss all the characteristics of the different stories that would make them enjoyable for others to read. Use the chart below to help you organize your ideas. Circle the reading of your choice. In the box to the left, write down the qualities that readers would enjoy about the first story. On the right, discuss qualities of the second story that the reader would enjoy. Then write an explanatory essay telling others all about your favorite author of multiple stories or pair of fantasy stories. Once you have gathered your information and facts, use the organizer below to map out your writing.

I suggest reading . . .

Adventure stories by...	Series of adventure fantasy stories...

I chose to write about _____

Fact 1

Fact 2

Fact 3

Fact 4

Fact 5

Write Your Essay!

Introduce your topic. Think of an exciting statement or question to pose to your audience that would make them want to read your essay.

_____

_____

_____

_____

_____

_____

_____

_____

Use facts and definitions to develop your story. Include a drawing or diagram that supports one of the facts.

_____

_____

_____

_____

_____

_____

_____

_____

_____

_____

Write your conclusion. Restate the facts and summarize the main points.

_____

_____

_____

_____

_____

_____

_____

_____

_____

Fables and Myths

In this unit, you will read fables and myths. A **fable** is a short story written in a simple way that teaches a moral or lesson. Fables often personify animals, trees, or rocks as main characters. A **myth** is a story that explains how things came to be. It can also express reasons for things that are difficult to explain. Traditionally, fables and myths were passed down in history by word of mouth. Today, there are a variety of fables and myths that have been put in writing for your enjoyment.

Put your imagination caps on, and let's begin!

Poseidon's Gifts

By Lisa McFarren

1   Earthquakes, shipwrecks, and storms at sea—Poseidon was the ancient Greek god of the ocean who had a bad temper and was not afraid to show it! When he was angry, he would throw down his trident—a long spear that had three sharp prongs—and split huge rocks in half. In great fear of him, people would offer a fat calf at a temple to please him. Sometimes it worked, and sometimes he became angrier.

2   One day, a king named Cecrops wanted to pick a patron god for the capital of the land of Attica. A patron god watches over the city to keep it safe. So Cecrops held a contest where the god who gave man the most useful gift would win this honor. Athena, the goddess of wisdom, gave the gift of an olive tree. Poseidon, wishing to outdo Athena, made a giant spring of water for people to drink. The spring wasn't very useful, however, because it had a salty taste just like the sea! Athena won the contest, and because the fruit of the olive tree was so good, the people named the capital Athens after her.

3   Poseidon grew hot with anger. He slammed his trident on the ground, which flooded all of Attica with seawater. People were very scared and ran to a high cliff for safety. The king of the gods, Zeus, came down from the sky to talk to Poseidon.

4   "Poseidon," Zeus said firmly. "Having people fear you is not how to get their love and respect. You must treat them nicely."

5   Poseidon stopped the flooding right away. He even created the horse for man to use. Poseidon would ride a horse himself, charging it across the water so each hoof shone brightly in the sunlight, just like the foam on an ocean wave.

Digging Deeper

Ancient Greek mythology is a treasure chest of storytelling. Long ago, people did not fully understand nature, so they created myths to explain the wonders of nature. You can do this, too!

UNDERSTANDING THE STORY

After reading "Poseidon's Gifts," answer the questions below.

1. Why did Cecrops hold the contest?

   A. To have the people name the city after Athena.

   B. To make sure the city would be safe.

   C. To make Athena give the city an olive tree.

   D. To offer a fat calf at a temple.

2. Match the names with their correct descriptions.

   A. Athena   1. a kingdom

   B. Athens   2 king of the land

   C. Attica   3. king of the gods

   D. Cecrops   4. god of the sea

   E. Poseidon   5. capital city

   F. Zeus   6. goddess of wisdom

Digging Deeper

Make a list of all the animals, birds, and plants that you find interesting. Then, do an Internet search to see if there is a myth, fable, or folktale about the plants and animals on your list (e.g., how the dog got its bark).

UNDERSTANDING CHARACTERS

1. List three examples of Poseidon's bad temper:

   A. _____

   B. _____

   C. _____

2. What did Poseidon do to make up for losing his temper?

   A. He said he wanted the people to love and respect him.

   B. He created the horse as a new gift to the people.

   C. He offered a fat calf to the people at the temple.

   D. He ran to a high cliff to be safe from the people.

PICTURES HELP WITH UNDERSTANDING

Look at these two pictures of Poseidon.

Illustration A

Illustration B

Activity 1

Fill out the Venn diagram for both pictures.

List the different details for each picture in their labeled circles. Then add any similar details in the middle of the diagram.

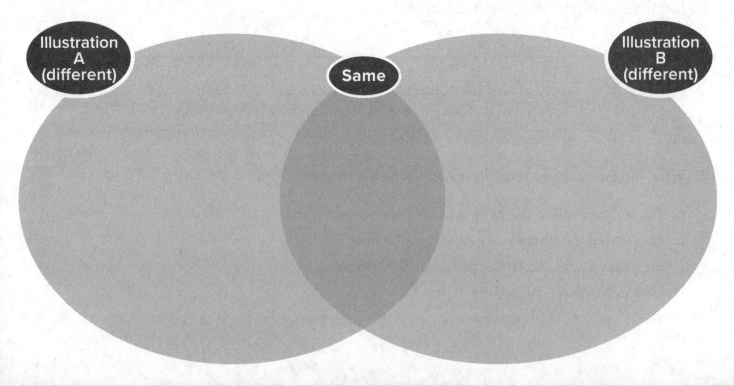

Activity 2

Which picture best shows the character of Poseidon in "Poseidon's Gifts"? Explain your answer.

_____

_____

_____

_____

USING REGULAR AND IRREGULAR NOUNS

Taking a singular noun and making it plural is usually a simple task. Add an "s" or "es" to the end of the word to accomplish this.

Irregular nouns are not that simple. While some types of irregular nouns follow some rules (and even those have exceptions!), many do not. The best way to learn these nouns is to memorize them.

> **Example:** Irregular nouns have many different spellings.
>
> For example, with irregular nouns that end in "f," you must first drop the "f." Then, add -ves to make the plural form of *hoof*.
>
> hoof – f ⟶ hoo + ves = hooves
>
> But not every noun that ends in "f" follows the rule above!

Change the nouns listed in the table below from singular to plural. Mark an "R" in the last column if they are regular nouns and an "I" if they are irregular.

Noun	Plural version	Type of noun (R or I)
Half	_____	_____
Cliff	_____	_____
Calf	_____	_____

USING ABSTRACT NOUNS

If you can't see it, smell it, touch it, feel it, or taste it, you are working with an abstract noun. The biggest challenge with abstract nouns is when you need to describe them.

Challenge: Read the abstract nouns below from "Poseidon's Gifts." Try to use them in a sentence without using a dictionary. When you are finished, you can check a dictionary to see how close you got to the real definition! Write a sentence using each word.

Noun: Wisdom

Definition: _____

Sentence: _____

_____

Noun: Fear

Definition: _____

Sentence: _____

_____

Noun: Honor

Definition: _____

Sentence: _____

_____

The Dog and His Reflection

An Aesop Fable

1   One day, Dog was walking by the butcher's store. The friendly butcher put down his large cleaver, which was as heavy as a brick, and smiled at Dog. He bent down and gave Dog a bone that was huge and meaty. Dog wagged his tail happily at the friendly butcher. He was very excited because it had been a very long time since he had such a special treat!

2   Dog headed straight home to eat his bone. The bone **promised** to be as tasty as pie. He was worried he might meet other dogs that would want to share it. He knew how greedy dogs could be! But to get home, he had to use a footbridge that crossed a very still, but wide stream. The stream was so still, it mirrored everything above it—the clouds, the sky, and the treetops. When Dog looked down, he saw his reflection in the quiet water. But Dog did not know he was looking at himself. He thought it was another dog—a dog with a huge, meaty bone!

3   Dog wanted that bone, too. At first he lifted his paw, but the "other dog" lifted its paw at the same time. Then Dog bit hard on his own bone and snarled while the other dog bit down hard on his bone and snarled too. Dog began to feel bothered. This very stubborn dog was not giving up his huge, meaty bone very easily at all! So Dog barked at the other dog to drop the bone. But when Dog opened his mouth, the bone fell into the quiet stream and made a huge *plop*! as it hit the water, sinking like a stone, never to be seen again.

UNDERSTANDING THE STORY

After reading "The Dog and His Reflection," answer the questions below.

Activity 1

1. Which is the **best** description of the "very stubborn dog"?

    A. It is a reflection of Dog.
    B. It is known to be greedy.
    C. It is heavy as a brick.
    D. It is feeling bothered by Dog.

2. Which phrase from the story tells the reader that the bone was very heavy?

    A. "huge and meaty"
    B. "such a special treat"
    C. "as heavy as a brick"
    D. "sinking like a stone"

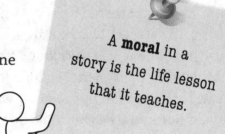

A **moral** in a story is the life lesson that it teaches.

Activity 2

1. What is the **moral** of the story?

    A. If you are carrying a special treat home, you should not stop for any reason.
    B. If you see your reflection in water, you should know who it is.
    C. If you try to take something that is not yours, you could lose everything.
    D. If you look down into a stream, you could drop a special treat in the water.

2. What detail from the story tells you the dog's actions were foolish?

    A. "But when Dog opened his mouth, the bone fell into the quiet stream . . . ."
    B. "He was worried he might meet other dogs who would want to share his bone."
    C. "When Dog looked down, he saw his reflection in the quiet water."
    D. "Then Dog bit hard on his own bone and snarled . . . ."

UNDERSTANDING THE CLUES

Read this sentence from the story.

*"The bone **promised** to be as tasty as pie."*

Ask yourself these questions to understand better how the word **promised** works in the sentence.

1. What does the word **promise** mean?

   _____
   _____
   _____

2. Can a bone promise something? Why or why not?

   _____
   _____
   _____

3. Would a bone be **tasty as pie** to you? Would it taste as good to a dog?

   _____
   _____
   _____

4. After answering these questions, explain what **promised** means in the sentence.

   _____
   _____
   _____

UNDERSTANDING REAL-LIFE CONNECTIONS IN WRITING

When you are reading a story, you may be able to make connections between the words you read and your own life. If a character in a story is **helpful**, think of a person you know who is helpful. If an experience was **exciting**, think about your own exciting experience. Doing this helps the reader to better understand words and how they are used in the text.

> **Example:**
> Word ⟶ helpful
>
> Real-life connection: My neighbor went out of her way to drive me to the library.
>
> Word ⟶ exciting
>
> Real-life connection: We enjoyed the baseball game last night. It went over nine innings!

Activity 1

Read these sentences from "The Dog and His Reflection."

*"The **friendly** butcher put down his large cleaver, which was as heavy as a brick, and smiled at Dog. He bent down and gave Dog a huge and meaty bone."*

The writer *says* the butcher is friendly, but how would a butcher *show* he is friendly? Explain.

_____

_____

Activity 2

Look at the words on the left. To the right, describe your own real-life connection to that word.

Word(s)	Real-Life Connection
stubborn	_____
happily	_____
greedily	_____

CHOOSING THE RIGHT WORDS

The way time is used in a story lets you know how important an event is.

Read the sentence from the story.

*"He was very excited because **it had been a very long time** since he had such a special treat!"*

How would the sentence read if the highlighted phrase was replaced with one of the clauses below? Would the dog have found it such a special treat after all?

1. it had been only a week

2. it had been an hour

3. it had been three years

WRITE YOUR OPINION

Everyone has an opinion—including you!

What is your opinion? Should you have to share something with your family or friends that was given to you as a gift? Write it down! Be sure you have a topic sentence (or main idea) that tells your opinion. Next, list three reasons why you should or should not share your gift with others. Remember to write a conclusion that sums up your ideas. Use the graphic organizer on the next page to help plan your idea.

WRITE YOUR OPINION

Plan an introduction, a body with your facts, and a conclusion before writing your essay. If you want to include a drawing or diagram, place it in the section with your reasons. Remember to use linking words *because, and,* and *also* to connect your opinions and reasons.

Introduction (Your opinion):

_____

_____

_____

Reason 1:

_____

_____

_____

Reason 2:

_____

_____

_____

Reason 3:

_____

_____

_____

Conclusion:

_____

_____

_____

Poetry

Reading poetry creates many bright pictures in your mind. Poetry uses metaphors, imagery, and symbolic language to describe experiences. It can stretch your imagination, forcing you to think outside of the box. When you figure out the meaning of difficult phrases or passages, you build your vocabulary and widen your thoughts. Poetry will also pull at your heartstrings because it is an expression of the way people feel.

Happy reading!

everyone is a poet

My Shadow

by Robert Louis Stevenson

I have a little shadow that goes in and out with me,
And what can be the use of him is more than I can see.
He is very, very like me from the heels up to the head;
And I see him jump before me, when I jump into my bed.

The funniest thing about him is the way he likes to grow—
Not at all like proper children, which is always very slow;
For he sometimes shoots up taller like an India-rubber ball,
And he sometimes gets so little that there's none of him at all.

He hasn't got a notion of how children ought to play,
And can only make a fool of me in every sort of way.
He stays so close beside me, he's a coward you can see;
I'd think shame to stick to nursie as that shadow sticks to me!

One morning, very early, before the sun was up,
I rose and found the shining dew on every buttercup;
But my lazy little shadow, like an arrant sleepy-head,
Had stayed at home behind me and was fast asleep in bed.

Digging Deeper

Poetry Read Aloud

Sometimes, you can get a better understanding of a poem by listening to the words being read aloud. With the help of an adult, listen to the reading of "My Shadow" by Robert Louis Stevenson once again. Tell about your favorite part and describe your own shadow.

UNDERSTANDING THE CLUES

Read these lines from "My Shadow." Answer the next three questions to better understand the highlighted phrases.

"*But **my lazy little shadow**, like an arrant sleepy-head,*

Had stayed at home behind me *and was fast asleep in bed.*"

1. Is the shadow a real person?

   _____

   _____

   _____

   _____

2. Can a shadow be lazy? Why or why not?

   _____

   _____

   _____

   _____

3. Identify at least two figurative phrases in the poem that are used to describe the speaker's shadow.

   _____

   _____

   _____

   _____

USING CONTEXT CLUES TO DETERMINE MEANING

Let's read this sentence.

*My dad had a hairy shadow from his **beard**; it was thick and covered most of his face.*

If you are not familiar with the word *beard*, you can look at the other words in the sentence to determine the meaning. Words and phrases such as *dad, hairy, thick,* and *covered most of his face* help you to understand that a beard is adult facial hair. These are called context clues.

Read the following lines from "My Shadow." Use the context clues in the lines to determine the meaning of the highlighted word or phrase. Write your responses on the lines below.

"One morning, very early, before the sun was up,
*I rose and found the **shining** dew on every buttercup;"*

Meaning: _____

*"**He hasn't got a notion** of how children ought to play,*
And can only make a fool of me in every sort of way."

Meaning: _____

*"But my lazy little shadow, like an **arrant** sleepy-head,*
Had stayed at home behind me and was fast asleep in bed."

Meaning: _____

Challenge: Write a short poem about your own shadow. How would you describe it? What does it look like? Remember to use expressive words and phrases that are both literal and figurative.

_____

_____

_____

_____

CHOOSING WORDS FOR EFFECT

Let's read this sentence.

The soothing rain with its gentle pitter-patter on my window sill made me forget about my troubling day at school.

How did you feel when you read this sentence? Was it calming? Words such as *soothing* and *gentle* help to create a relaxing effect on the reader.

When you are writing, choose words or phrases carefully to be sure that you are using the correct one to express your desired effect.

Activity 1

Read this line from the poem.

*"He is **very, very** like me from the heels up to the head;"*

Which word could replace the highlighted phrase and still have the same effect?

    A. exactly

    B. almost

    C. nothing

    D. carefully

Activity 2

In the poem "My Shadow," the author uses certain words and phrases to characterize the shadow. In doing so, the reader has a specific understanding of the effects of the boy's shadow. Select the words or phrases that the author uses to describe the shadow, both physically and emotionally.

The Shadow	Words or Phrases
Physical qualities of the shadow	
Emotional qualities of the shadow	

In this lesson, you will read two poems about nature.

Autumn

by Emily Dickinson

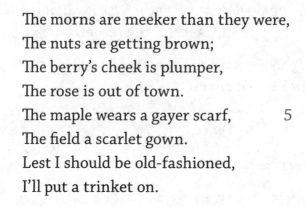

The morns are meeker than they were,
The nuts are getting brown;
The berry's cheek is plumper,
The rose is out of town.
The maple wears a gayer scarf,   5
The field a scarlet gown.
Lest I should be old-fashioned,
I'll put a trinket on.

Afternoon on a Hill

by Edna St. Vincent Millay

I WILL be the gladdest thing
   Under the sun!
I will touch a hundred flowers
   And not pick one.

I will look at cliffs and clouds   5
   With quiet eyes,
Watch the wind bow down the grass,
   And the grass rise.

And when lights begin to show
   Up from the town,   10
I will mark which must be mine,
   And then start down!

UNDERSTANDING THE POEM

Answer these questions that are based on the poem "Autumn."

1. Based on the poem, list at least two characteristics of autumn.

_____

_____

_____

_____

2. Which statement **best** describes fall mornings?

    A. They are a lot colder.

    B. They are much more calm and gentle.

    C. They are shorter than summer mornings.

    D. They are longer than any other season.

Answer this question about the poem "Afternoon on a Hill."

3. What makes the author of the poem truly happy? Support your answer with line(s) from the poem.

_____

_____

_____

_____

Digging Deeper

Autumn in the United States

There are many beautiful sights in nature. As Dickinson's poem highlights the images of fall, expand your knowledge by learning the science behind the changing colors of autumn. Discuss your findings with an adult or a friend.

UNDERSTANDING THE CLUES

Answer these questions that are based on the poem "Autumn."

Activity 1

1. Read line 3 from the poem.

   "The berry's cheek is plumper."

   What does this line really mean? Why is this a nonliteral statement?

   _____

   _____

2. Read line 4 from the poem.

   "The rose is out of town."

   Which **best** describes the meaning of this line?

   A. The rose walked away from the forest.
   B. Roses do not like the fall weather.
   C. Summer is over because there are no more roses.
   D. The rose is going on vacation.

When a statement is **literal**, we understand it just how it is written.

When a statement is **nonliteral**, it means something other than the exact words in it.

Activity 2

Look at these phrases from "Afternoon on a Hill." Decide whether each phrase is literal or nonliteral and circle L or NL. If the phrase is nonliteral, write its true meaning on the line.

1. *"I will touch a hundred flowers*
   And not pick one."

   L or NL   Meaning: _____

2. *"Watch the wind bow down the grass,*
   And the grass rise."

   L or NL   Meaning: _____

PARTS OF A POEM

Review the stanzas in the poem "Afternoon on a Hill" to answer the questions below.

1. In "Afternoon on a Hill," the poet uses the first two stanzas to describe happiness with nature. What interesting things do you learn in the last stanza?

   _____

   _____

   _____

   _____

   _____

   _____

   _____

2. How do the first two stanzas affect the last stanza? Use the space below to write a paragraph. Be sure to use examples from the poem in your response.

   _____

   _____

   _____

   _____

   _____

   _____

   _____

   _____

   _____

PARTS OF SPEECH AND THEIR FUNCTIONS

Nouns are people, places, or things. Pronouns take the place of nouns and can also show more than one person, place, or thing. Verbs express the actions of the nouns. Adjectives are words that describe a noun. Adverbs describe verbs more deeply by saying how, when, where, or why. All of these parts of speech have different functions. It is important to know their roles in different sentences.

The activities below ask you to either *change* something in the sentence or *to answer a question* about the sentence.

1. The following sentence contains a *noun*. How would you change the sentence to say **three or more people went to pick flowers?**

   Mom and I went to pick flowers.

   _____

2. **Insert a verb** into the sentence below.

   Devin watched as the bird _____ through the air.

3. **Adjectives** describe nouns. **Put an adjective** into the sentence below.

   The _____ sun was shining in our faces.

4. How would you change the sentence to **describe the action more deeply?**

   Dad raked the leaves into a pile.

   _____

5. Tell **what part of speech each underlined word represents and its function**.

   Ashley was so excited about her nature walk coming up next week that she happily jumped up and down for joy.

   Ashley _____   excited _____

   her _____   next week _____

   happily _____   jumped _____

WRITE YOUR OPINION

Get ready—your science class is going on a nature walk! The teacher has instructed everyone to write an opinion essay stating why the class should go to a place of his or her own choice. Think about it. Where should your class go so that everyone can enjoy a wonderful outdoor experience? To a park? To a beach? To the mountains?

In the graphic organizer below, write an opinion essay on why your class should take a nature walk to the place of your choice. If necessary, ask an adult to help as you research on the Internet about your choice. Look for facts and information to support why the place you chose is a good location for a nature walk.

State your opinion. Where should your class go for the nature walk?

_____

_____

_____

_____

Describe the benefits of the place that you have chosen. What are some things that you can learn, see, and do here?

1. _____

_____

_____

2. _____

_____

_____

3. _____

_____

_____

WRITE YOUR OPINION

Use your outline from page 133 to develop your story below.

Introduction (Opinion sentence):

_____

_____

_____

_____

Body (Describe why the class should go to the place of your choice):

_____

_____

_____

_____

_____

_____

_____

Conclusion (Restate your opinion):

_____

_____

_____

_____

Remember to use your *My Journal* pages at the back of the workbook if you need more space to write.

REVIEW

Reading Fluency

Adults: Time your student reading aloud for one minute. Make a note of where your student is at the end of one minute. (Your student should be able to read between 90 and 110 words per minute.) Have your student continue reading to the end of the passage in order to answer the questions on the following page.

The Tortoise and the Ducks
An Aesop Fable

The Tortoise, you know, carries his house on his back. No matter how hard he tries, he	17
cannot leave home. They say that Jupiter punished him so, because he was such a lazy	33
stay-at-home that he would not go to Jupiter's wedding, even when especially invited.	46
After many years, Tortoise began to wish he had gone to that wedding. When he saw how	63
gaily the birds flew about and how the Hare and the Chipmunk and all the other animals	80
ran nimbly by, always eager to see everything there was to be seen, the Tortoise felt very	97
sad and discontented. He wanted to see the world too, and there he was with a house on	115
his back and little short legs that could hardly drag him along.	127
One day he met a pair of Ducks and told them all his trouble.	141
"We can help you to see the world," said the Ducks. "Take hold of this stick with your	159
teeth and we will carry you far up in the air where you can see the whole countryside.	177
But keep quiet or you will be sorry."	185
The Tortoise was very glad indeed. He seized the stick firmly with his teeth, the two	201
Ducks took hold of it one at each end, and away they sailed up toward the clouds. Just	219
then a Crow flew by. He was very much astonished at the strange sight and cried, "This	236
must surely be the King of Tortoises!"	243
"Why certainly—" began the Tortoise.	248
But as he opened his mouth to say these foolish words, he lost his hold on the stick,	266
and down he fell to the ground.	273

Words read in 1 minute – errors = WPM

135

Activity 1

Read the sentences from the passage in the left column. Then, look at the underlined word(s). Use what you know about nouns, pronouns, verbs, adjectives, and adverbs to complete the rest of the chart. Be sure to identify the underlined word's part of speech and its function in the sentence.

Sentence	Part of Speech	Function
They say that Jupiter punished him so, because he was such a lazy stay-at-home that he would not go to Jupiter's wedding, even when <u>especially</u> invited.		
He wanted to see the world too, and there he was with a house on his back and <u>little short</u> legs that could hardly drag him along.		
He <u>seized</u> the stick firmly with his teeth, the two Ducks took hold of it one at each end, and away they sailed up toward the clouds.		

Nouns, pronouns, verbs, adjectives, and adverbs:

Noun: A person, place, or thing.

Pronoun: A word that takes the place of a noun, like he, she, etc....

Adjective: A word that describes a noun.

Adverb: A word that changes, describes, or simplifies the meaning of a verb, an adjective, or another adverb.

Activity 2

Use what you know about regular (R) and irregular (I) plural nouns to fill in the table below.

> **Regular noun:** Noun that is made plural by simply adding -*s* or -*es* to the end of the word.
>
> **Irregular noun:** When a noun does not follow the standard rules to become plural; for example: *knife* becomes *knives*.

Noun	Plural version	Type of noun (R or I)
1. tooth		
2. wedding		
3. bird		
4. ground		

Activity 3

Underline the abstract nouns in the following sentences.

> **Abstract noun:** A type of noun that refers to something which a person cannot touch: an idea, a concept, a feeling, or a quality.

1. The tortoise's lazy attitude was the reason why he had to carry his shell everywhere.

2. Jupiter did not show any compassion toward the tortoise.

3. Astonishment fell upon the tortoise as Crow flew by him.

Let's apply the reading skills you covered in this section.

The Fox and the Stork

An Aesop Fable

1   The Fox one day thought of a plan to amuse himself at the expense of the Stork, at whose odd appearance he was always laughing.

2   "You must come and dine with me today," he said to the Stork, smiling to himself at the trick he was going to play. The Stork gladly accepted the invitation and arrived in good time and with a very good appetite.

3   For dinner, the Fox served soup. But it was set out in a very shallow dish, and all the Stork could do was to wet the very tip of his bill. Not a drop of soup could he get. But the Fox lapped it up easily, and, to increase the disappointment of the Stork, made a great show of enjoyment.

4   The hungry Stork was much displeased at the trick, but he was a calm, even-tempered fellow and saw no good in flying into a rage. Instead, not long afterward, he invited the Fox to dine with him in turn. The Fox arrived promptly at the time that had been set, and the Stork served a fish dinner that had a very appetizing smell. But it was served in a tall jar with a very narrow neck. The Stork could easily get at the food with his long bill, but all the Fox could do was to lick the outside of the jar, and sniff at the delicious odor. And when the Fox lost his temper, the Stork just looked at him calmly and didn't say a word.

Anansi and the Turtle

A Poem Based on a Nigerian Fable

1   Anansi the spider baked yams galore,
tasty and yummy from his garden.
He was just about to eat them,
when he heard a loud "knock, knock!" at the door.

2   It was Turtle, who must have smelled the food.
Tired and hungry
Turtle asked Anansi to share the yams,
"I'm starving, dear Anansi, and your meal looks so good."

3   Anansi was greedy and didn't want to share.
So he thought up a plan to trick Turtle,
Anansi asked Turtle to come in,
"Sit down, help yourself, and have a chair."

4   Before they ate, Turtle went to the river to wash hands.
While he was gone,
Anansi started eating the yams.
"I didn't want these tasty treats to go to waste, you see."

5   Turtle left the house still hungry with one last word to say.
He was polite as can be to Anansi,
and he offered a deal he could not refuse.
"If ever you are hungry and in need of food, swing by my way."

6 Later that week, Anansi needed some food.
He remembered Turtle offered a free dinner,
smelled a delicious stew brewing
and decided that Turtle's offer would still be good.

7 Turtle asked Anansi to join him at the table,
However, the meal was underwater.
Anansi tried to swim down to eat
But he was so light that he wasn't able.

8 Turtle kept eating so happy and carefree.
But he did not feel bad for Anansi at all.
"I just outsmarted the clever spider,
while he thought that he could only outsmart me!"

Use what you learned from Units 7 and 8 to answer the questions about the selections above.

1. In "The Fox and the Stork," why was the stork angry at the fox?

_____

_____

_____

2. In "Anansi and the Turtle," what trick does Anansi play on the turtle?

_____

_____

_____

3. In "Anansi and the Turtle," why was the spider unable to eat his meal?

_____

_____

_____

4. In "Anansi and the Turtle," what does stanza 3 reveal about Anansi that affects the rest of the poem?

_____

_____

_____

5. What lesson is learned from "The Fox and the Stork" and "Anansi and the Turtle"?

_____

_____

_____

6. Explain how both authors use details to convey those lessons.

_____

_____

_____

7. Using the pictures from "The Fox and the Stork," how does it help you understand the action of the story?

_____

_____

_____

8. If you were going to add to the picture for the poem "Anansi and the Turtle," what details would you add to help the reader better understand what is happening in the story?

_____

_____

_____

_____

DISCOVER

Write Your Opinion

Writing an opinion essay allows you to express your own point of view. An opinion is a belief or feeling that must be supported by your reasons for them.

In these units, you read myths, fables, and poems. All of these have morals, or lessons that the author is trying to teach the reader. Think about one of the lessons you learned from these reading selections. Write an opinion essay explaining why you think it's important to follow the story's moral or lesson in real life. Be sure to include examples from the reading selection.

State your opinion. (I learned an important lesson from reading _____.
The moral, or lesson, is . . .)

_____

_____

_____

_____

_____

_____

_____

_____

_____

_____

_____

Describe in detail why this lesson is important in real life.

_____

_____

_____

_____

_____

_____

_____

_____

Describe the benefits of the lesson and how they apply to real life.

1. _____

_____

_____

_____

2. _____

_____

_____

_____

3. _____

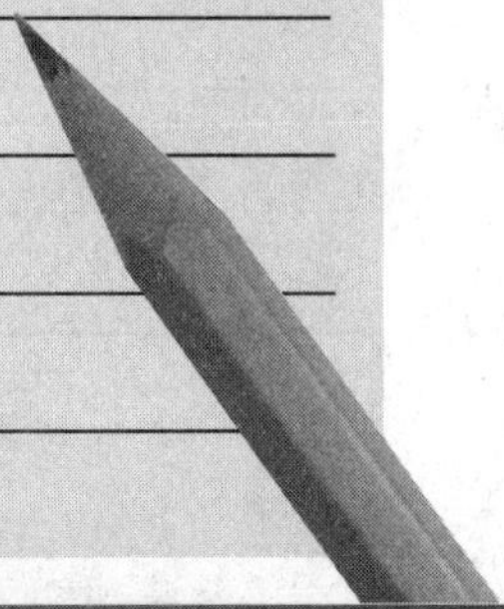

_____

_____

_____

Write Your Essay

Use your outline from pages 142–143 to develop your essay below.

Introduction (Opinion sentence): _____

_____

_____

_____

_____

Body (Describe the moral or lesson from one reading selection and explain why it's

important): _____

_____

_____

_____

_____

_____

_____

_____

_____

_____

_____

Conclusion (Restate your opinion): _____

_____

_____

_____

_____

_____

_____

My Journal

My Journal

My Journal

My Journal

My Journal

My Journal

My Journal

My Journal

Answer Key

Reading Foundational Skills

Unit 1—Fluency: Read with Purpose and Understanding

Lesson 1—The Family Camping Adventure

Page 5. 1. Jason sees the perfect spot while mom is driving; 2. The tent is yellow and green, and shaped like a triangle. It is big enough to hold three people. The tent has netting that goes all the way around to keep mosquitoes out; 3. The kids like camping. Some evidence to support this could be Jason helping to find the campsite, Tanya and Jason helping to unpack, and Tanya getting excited about the s'mores; 4. S'mores are sandwich treats made of marshmallows, graham crackers, and chocolate. Tanya is very excited to eat the s'mores. The author helps the reader to understand this by using an exclamation mark and the word "Hooray."

Lesson 2—Good Friends

Page 7. 1. Marla told Amanda she did not want to be her friend anymore; 2. Marla's dog, Tank, makes her laugh because he is licking away her tears and has bad breath; 3. The author says Tank is wagging his tail back and forth; 4. Marla is angry with Amanda and so she is mean to her. She yells at her, "I don't want to be your friend anymore!" The expression in her voice is mean.

Lesson 3—Ready, Set, Dig!

Page 9. 1. According to the article, after finding an artifact, the digger takes it to the lab to study it; 2. The author states that if you like digging in the dirt, you could very well become an archaeologist in the future; 3. The word *excavate* means "to **dig**"—a process archaeologists use to find artifacts; 4. To inform kids about archaeology

Lesson 4—How to Play Checkers

Page 11. 1. People have been playing checkers for hundreds of years, since the times of ancient Egypt; 2. The author helps the reader to understand how to play checkers by including step-by-step instructions and pictures to help the reader visualize the actual board game; 3. The author uses an exclamation mark to show excitement; 4. The game is finished when one player has no more checkers on the board.

Reading and Writing: Informational Texts

Unit 2—American Athletes

Lesson 1—Babe Ruth

Page 16. Finding the Main Idea and Details: 1. C; 2. C; 3. Answers will vary. Sample response: After Ruth began playing for the Yankees, he set home run records, had high batting averages, and even set records for attracting the most people to attend his games. In 1920, when Ruth first joined the Yankees, over one million people came to watch the games during that season.; 4. C

Page 17. Relationships Between Events: 1. Effect: He was so pleased that the Orioles signed Ruth to a baseball contract; 2. Effect: As a result, he set home run records and had a high batting average; 3. Cause: In 1920, Ruth hit more home runs (54) than any other American League player; 4. Cause: Ruth held the record for the most home runs.

Page 18. Verb Tenses Activity 1: 1. The player will swing the bat; 2. The girl will go to the baseball game; Activity 2: 1. past; 2. future; 3. past; 4. present

Page 19. Using Commas and Quotation Marks: 1. George said, "I want to play baseball." 2. "He hit a home run!" screamed the coach; 3. She stated, "I would like to play baseball." 4. "Can we go to the baseball field today?" Todd asked; 5. Serena interrupted excitedly, "I know that we are going to win!" 6. "How old is your friend?" asked the little girl. "Old enough to play in the game," said the little boy; 7. "I saw the ball fly over the fence," said Sunaya. "How many times did that happen?" asked Lelani; Challenge: Answers will vary. Example: "Mr. Ruth, when you hit that ball over the fence, I was amazed! I will never forget the way the crowd cheered," said Brad. "I love this game, and I love to win," replied Babe.

Lesson 2—A Champion Above the Rest

Page 21. Mapping the Main Idea and Supporting Details: Answers will vary. Sample response: Main idea—Serena Williams is one of the best tennis players in the world; Supporting detail 1: Serena Williams has won a total of 641

tennis matches; Supporting detail 2: Serena won a total of 39 grand slams. Supporting detail 3: Serena changed the world of tennis because she never gave up.

Page 22. Different Points of View: 1. D; 2. Answers will vary. Sample response: Yes, I agree that Serena is a tennis champion because she won 641 tennis matches and 39 grand slams.

Pages 22–23. Determining Meaning: 1. D; 2. D

Page 24. Verb Tenses: 1. We watched the World Tennis Championship on television; The player learned a new way to hit the ball; 2. A. rode; B. bought; C. became; D. taught

Page 25. Vocabulary Development and Use: 1. athlete; 2. inner strength; 3. practice; 4. force; Challenge: Answers will vary. Example: My uncle Misael is a professional football player. He has been practicing since he was a young boy. He is known for kicking the ball with a lot of force. Last year he broke his arm and went on to win seven out of ten games. This showed that Misael has inner strength. I am proud of my uncle. He is a great athlete!

Page 26. Spelling Patterns: 1. knee; 2. night; 3. write; 4. sign; Challenge: Answers will vary. Example: My mom knows I want a puppy. She says he will gnaw on everything. If I get a puppy I will wrap him in a blanket and hold him tight.

Stop and Think! Units 1–2 Review

Page 29. Activity 1: 1. Past: Many people watched the Olympics. Future: Many people will watch the Olympics; 2. Past: The instructor trained the students for the Olympic trials. Future: The instructor will train the students for the Olympic trials; 3. Past: Jason and his two brothers took exercise classes at the YMCA. Future: Jason and his two brothers will take exercises classes at the YMCA; 4. Past: My friend played soccer in the 2012 Olympic games in London. Future: My friend will play soccer in the 2012 Olympic games in London; Activity 2: 1. "It's time to put your sneakers on," said Dad; 2. Jamaeka replied, "One of the ancient Greek gods was named Zeus"; 3. "Are you going to enter the bicycle competition?" asked the instructor; 4. The teacher told her students, "Take out your tennis rackets and begin practicing."; Activity 3: 1. Answers will vary. Example: I went to the circus and saw clowns juggling balls. When I went home, I tried to juggle balls at home with my family; 2. They would need to practice a lot and be very strong.

Stop and Think! Units 1–2 Understand

Page 31. 1. The main idea is that Usain Bolt is the fastest runner in the world; 2. One key detail to support this is Usain Bolt holds the world record for the fastest foot speed.

Another example is that he ran in the 100-meter dash in 9.58 seconds. He holds the world record. Another example is Bolt is the first man to win the 100- and 200-meter races in the Olympics; 3. He earned the nickname *Lightning Bolt* because of the pose he takes after he finishes a race and for his fast feet; 4. Answers may vary. Acceptable choices must have something with speed or racing in them. Another possible title for this article is: "The World's Fastest Man"; 5. A; 6. Answers may vary. Acceptable choices must have something with his records, winning, or the foundation. Usain Bolt became a legend when he became the first man to hold both medals at the 2008 Olympics.

Unit 3—Migration

Lesson 1—Up and Away!

Page 36. Understanding Vocabulary: 1. C; 2. C; 3. A

Page 37. Describing Relationships Activity 1: 1. long; 2. short; 3. medium; Activity 2: 1. They need to find food and places to have their babies; 2. Birds are attracted to lights; 3. Birds have a special mineral in their noses.

Page 38. Understanding Text Features: 1. D; 2. A; 3. D; 4. It describes the picture.

Page 39. Understanding Pronouns Activity 1: 1. him; 2. their; 3. their; 4. we; Activity 2: our, We, us, they, them

Page 40. Types of Sentences Activity 1: 1. compound; 2. complex; 3. simple; 4. complex; 5. compound; Activity 2: Answers will vary. I read a book about bird migration. (S) I read a book about bird migration, and my brother watched a movie. (C) We visited the bird museum and went bird watching before the season was over. (CP)

Lesson 2—A Butterfly Above the Rest

Page 42. Determining Meaning Activity 1: 1. B; 2. B; 3. A

Page 43. Describing Connections: 1. D; 2. B

Page 44. Comparing and Contrasting Articles: Same— Both butterflies and birds migrate to find food and nesting locations. They both use earth's features to find their way when they migrate; they both face problems when migrating that could kill them; Monarch—no other animal on earth migrates farther. Birds—have different types of migration: short, medium, and long.

Page 45. Using Suffixes Activity 1: 1. butterflies; 2. slowly; 3. tried; 4. injured; 5. cloudy; 6. moving; Activity 2: Answers will vary. Sample responses: 1. careless; 2. forgetfulness; 3. flying

Page 46. Prefixes or Suffixes: 1. without clouds; 2. plans; 3. very gently; 4. without motion; 5. not thinking; Challenge: Answers will vary: 1. incurable—cannot be cured; 2. disagree—to fail to agree, have a different opinion; 3. pretest—a test that comes before and prepares me for the real test

Unit 4—Nutrition and Exercise

Lesson 1—Healthy Eating

Page 50. Understanding Connections: 1. Vitamin A—healthy eyes; Vitamin D—helps the body use calcium; Vitamin C—healthy immune system; Vitamin K—helps for normal blood clotting; Vitamin B—brain health; Vitamin E—helps the body make red blood cells

Page 51. Determining Meanings: 1. C; 2. A; 3. B; 4. B

Page 52. Pictures Help with Understanding: 1. C; 2. Nutrition label 1 is higher in fat grams with a total of 13.6 grams; 3. B; 4. Nutrition label 2 is the healthier choice. It contains more vitamins and less sugar and fat.

Page 53. Different Types of Adjectives Activity 1: 1. healthier; 2. sweetest

Page 54. Activity 2: 1. newest; 2. freshest; 3. riper; 4. cheaper; 5. friendliest; Capitalizing Titles: 1. W and A should be crossed out; 2. H and R should be circled; 3. The V should be circled; 4. U, I, and T should be crossed out; Challenge: Answers will vary. One example is: The Biggest Carrot on a Farm.

Lesson 2—Get Up and Move!

Page 57. Activity 1 (Crossword): 1. strength; 2. flexibility; 3. disease; 4. endurance; 5. joints; 6. surfing the Web; 7. muscles; 8. exercise; 9. bones

Page 58. Answers will vary. Title: Get Up and Move!; Topic: Exercise; The author of the text believes that all children should exercise more and that things like watching TV and sitting too long take away from the time you could use to exercise. The author also feels that exercise is healthy for you; I believe exercise is good for you. I believe this because I feel better when I exercise.

Page 59. Activity 1: How to Use Commas: Cojack, MO; Venus, Wyoming; Summerton, Wyoming; Orlando, Florida; Drive, Venus, WY; Activity 2: Answers will vary. New York, NY; 321 Main Street, Chocolate Town, VA 20442

Page 60. Telescope—a device shaped like a long tube that you look through in order to see things that are far away; microscope—a tool used for producing a much larger view of very small objects so that they can be seen clearly; kaleidoscope—a tube that has mirrors and loose pieces of colored glass or plastic inside at one end so that you see many different patterns when you turn the tube while looking in through the other end; stethoscope—an instrument that is used for listening to someone's heart or lungs

Page 61. Activity 2: Answers will vary: microphone—an instrument that makes sound louder; saxophone—a woodwind instrument; phonics—the sounds that letters make; homophones—words that have the same sound but different meanings

Stop and Think! Units 3–4 Review

Page 64. Activity 1: 1. Marley the Magnificent Butterfly; 2. From Caterpillar to Butterfly; 3. A World of Butterflies; 4. My, Oh My—A Butterfly; Activity 2: 1. I like to catch and watch butterflies with my friends; 2. The students are studying about chrysalises. They have a test tomorrow; 3. I tried to teach my friend about caterpillars while my friend tried to teach me about ladybugs; Activity 3: 1. Friendship means the state of being someone's friend. Students may supply a sentence to help them explain the meaning; 2. Excitement means being excited. Students may supply a sentence to help them explain the meaning; 3. Colorful means something is full of color. Students may supply a sentence to help them explain the meaning.

Stop and Think! Units 3–4 Understand

Pages 66–67. 1. Step 1: Find a spot where plants can receive lots of sun; Step 2: Put down fresh soil; Step 3: Dig deep holes and plant seeds; Step 4: Water the plants every day; 2. The result of Natasha's idea is that she and her dad grew vegetables; 3. I think the author is trying to convince me to eat more vegetables; 4. I think growing my own vegetables is best because the food will be very fresh. Also, my parents would not have to go to the grocery store as much with food growing in our own backyard; 5. The illustration of the plate relates to the text in paragraph 1. It shows me a picture of the plate where the vegetables are just a little bit bigger than fruit; 6. The plate gives me information about the kinds of food I should eat.

Reading and Writing: Literature

Unit 5—Author Study: Adventures in Fantasy

Lesson 1—Alice's Adventures in Wonderland

Page 75. Describing Characters: 1. C; 2. A

Pages 76–77. Pictures Help with Understanding: 1. Answers may vary, but students may say that Alice has an annoyed expression. She does not seem to be enjoying the party; 2. Answers may vary, but students may say that the tea party is not very fun. The mood is tense; 3. Answers may vary, but students may say that if Alice were smiling, she would be enjoying the tea party.

Pages 78–79. The Effect of Words and Shades of Meaning: 1. Answers may vary, but students may say that "tossing" can make you think of someone swinging his or her hair back; 2. Answers may vary, but students may say that "shaking" is more active than "tossing," and that people shake their heads when they are saying "no." "Moving" does not give a strong image at all because a head can move different ways; Challenge: 1. C; 2. D; 3. A; 4. B

Lesson 2—Through the Looking-Glass

Page 83. Understanding the Story: 1. B; 2. D

Page 84. Comparing and Contrasting Stories: 1. Answers will vary, but students may say that both stories have Alice in them and that Alice meets characters who talk nonsense; 2. Answers may vary, but students may say that one story has a tea party where a talking rabbit is present and where the Hatter talks about Time as if it were a person. The other story has a talking egg that changes the definitions of words when he wants to.

Page 85. Understanding Possessives: 1. A. year's; B. book's; C. adjectives'; D. stories'; 2. A. Alice's; B. Humpty Dumpty's; C. word's; D. Lewis Carroll's. Using Reference Material: B. confused

Unit 6—Books by the Same Author
Lesson 1—A Little Princess

Page 90. Understanding the Story: 1. A; 2. C; 3. "The school ought to be very fashionable now Miss Minchin has a princess for a pupil." "She had meant it to be rather a secret, and here was Lavinia deriding it before nearly all the school." Describing Characters: 1. C; 2. B

Page 91. Understanding the Parts of a Story: 1. The first paragraph shows that Lavinia wants to start a fight and sets up the drama of the story; 2. The fourth paragraph is important to the passage because Sara explains why she pretends to be a princess. The story would not make sense if it were left out; 3. The story would not be as dramatic because it would show that the girls were siding with Sara at the beginning of the fight.

Page 92. Different Points of View Activity 1: 1. Yes; Students should circle the following words: *she, she, her, her*; 2. "When I spoke it was in a quiet, steady voice; I held my head up, and everybody listened to me;" Activity 2: Answers will vary, but students may say that Sara is feeling upset and embarrassed.

Page 94. Connecting Words Activity 1: 1. so; 2. but; 3. for; 4. and; Activity 2: 1. C; 2. A

Lesson 2—The Secret Garden

Page 96. Understanding the Story: 1. Correct order—4, 3, 1, 2; 2. A missel thrush is a bird. The word "nest" is a clue given to help the reader; 3. Mary describes the coming of spring in the following: "It is the sun shining on the rain and the rain falling on the sunshine, and things pushing up and working under the earth."

Page 97. Describing Characters: 1. C; 2. B

Page 98. Comparing and Contrasting Stories by the Same Author: 1. Answers may vary, but students may say that both stories involve girls who have a secret; 2.Answers may vary, but students may say that in *A Little Princess*, Sara is upset because her secret is revealed, but in *The Secret Garden*, Mary wants to share her secret with Colin.

Page 99. Changing Word Endings: 1. butterflies; 2. cities; 3. pansies

Page 100. Word Families: Answers may vary, but word families should be listed in each box (e.g., Day—pay, say, way; Nest—best, chest, west; Slip—flip, dip, chip).

Stop and Think! Units 5–6 Review

Page 104. Activity 1: Answers will vary, but students should correctly use one of the subordinating conjunctions in each sentence; 1. Although I like playing in the snow, I hate the bitter cold. I will play the game as long as I do not have to sing; Activity 2: Answers will vary, but student should correctly punctuate the possessive noun(s) in each sentence; 1. Seth's winter jacket was too small for him, so his mother bought him a new one. 2. Until the students' school is rebuilt, they will have classes at the YMCA. Activity 3: 1. happy; 2. skipped; 3. cries; 4. Answers will vary, but student should choose a word that uses the suffix *–ist*. Example: Archaeologist: An archaeologist is an expert in studying things from the past; 5. Answers will vary, but student should choose a word that uses the suffix *–ness*. Example: Kindness is the state of being kind. The boy showed kindness by helping the girl plant flowers in the garden.

Stop and Think! Units 5–6 Understand

Page 107. 1. The Lion has no courage. He is a coward; 2. He is ashamed of being a coward; 3. His crying makes the other characters feel sorry for him and want to help him. In turn, when they talk about going to Oz, he wants to join them so he can get a little bit of courage; 4. Paragraph two explains why the Lion roars, and also why he is so ashamed. He says the other animals expect him to be the King of Beasts, but he is afraid. The reader now sees the Lion as a sympathetic character; 5. The Scarecrow and Dorothy give the Lion the best advice. If they were not in the story, the conversation between the Lion and the Tin Woodman would not resolve the Lion's problem; 6. Sad

Unit 7—Fables and Myths

Lesson 1—Poseidon's Gifts

Page 113. Understanding the Story: 1. B; 2. A. 6; B. 5; C. 1; D. 2; E. 4; F. 3; Understanding Characters: 1. Answers will vary, but students may include that Poseidon created earthquakes, shipwrecks, and storms at sea; he started a bad flood; he slammed his trident down; 2. B

Page 114. Pictures Help with Understanding Activity 1: Answers will vary, but students may describe Illustration A as being more serious and Illustration B as being more silly. A similar detail from both illustrations is of Poseidon holding a trident.

Page 115. Activity 2: Students should pick Illustration A. Poseidon is characterized in the story as serious and mean, not fun-loving like Illustration B; Using Regular and Irregular Nouns: halves, I; cliffs, R; calves or calfs, I or R

Page 116. Using Abstract Nouns: Wisdom: Knowledge gained through experience; My teacher has a lot of wisdom. Fear: A feeling of being in danger; I fear a tornado is coming. Honor: Recognition; People should show honor to a king.

Lesson 2—The Dog and His Reflection

Page 118. Understanding the Story Activity 1: 1. A; 2. D; Activity 2: 1. C; 2. A

Page 119. Understanding the Clues: 1. Students should be able to define "promise"; 2. No. Answers will vary; 3. No. Yes; 4. Answers will vary but should reflect students' understanding of figurative language.

Page 120. Understanding Real-Life Connections in Writing Activity 1: The butcher "smiled" at Dog. He gave Dog "a huge and meaty bone"; Activity 2: Answers will vary. Sample: My brother can be very stubborn about sharing his toys. I would happily share my toys with a friend. I would not greedily keep them for myself.

Page 121. Choosing the Right Words: 1. Maybe not; 2. Probably not; 3. Definitely yes

Unit 8—Poetry

Lesson 1—My Shadow

Page 125. Understanding the Clues: 1. No, the shadow is not a real person. The author of the poem made the shadow seem like a real person to show how interested and annoyed the young boy is with this part of himself that he cannot get rid of; 2. A shadow cannot literally be lazy because it is not human. Laziness is a human characteristic and therefore this statement is nonliteral; 3. Answers will vary. Two examples: "For he sometimes shoots up taller like an India-rubber ball"; "He stays close beside me, he's a coward you can see."

Page 126. Using Context Clues to Determine Meaning: shining—bright; "He hasn't got a notion"—He doesn't have a clue; arrant—the worst kind of sleepy head or being really bad. Challenge: Answers will vary. Student must use expressive words and literal and nonliteral language.

Page 127. Choosing Words for Effect Activity 1: A; Activity 2: Physical qualities of the shadow—shoots up tall like a rubber ball; sometimes very little; same movements as boy (jumps); Emotional qualities of the shadow—coward; sometimes stays behind

Lesson 2—Autumn/Afternoon on a Hill

Page 129. Understanding the Poem: 1. Nuts get darker and the field changes to scarlet; 2. B; 3. The speaker of the poem is truly happy being under the sun (lines 1–2 state, "I WILL be the gladdest thing/Under the sun!").

Page 130. Understanding the Clues Activity 1: 1. This statement is nonliteral because berries really don't have cheeks. It means that the fall berries are growing plump; 2. C; Activity 2: 1. L; 2. NL (This means that even though someone may be small and weak like grass, a person can still be strong and get up again even after being knocked down.)

Page 131. Parts of a Poem: Answers will vary. Sample student response: 1. In the last stanza of "Afternoon on a Hill," I learn that the poet is sitting on a hill watching the sunset over the city in which he lives. 2. In "Afternoon on a Hill," the first two stanzas affect the last stanza. In the first two stanzas, the poet discusses what he or she loves about nature: the sun, flowers, and independence of the grass. However, in the last stanza, the reader learns that the poet is up high and staring down at nature. The poet wants to be a part of nature and can't wait to actually be in its presence.

Page 132. Parts of Speech and Their Functions: 1. We went to pick flowers; 2. Devin watched as the bird flew through the air; 3. The bright sun was shining in our faces; 4. Dad carefully raked the leaves into a pile; 5. noun; adverb; pronoun; adjective; adverb; verb

Stop and Think! Units 7–8 Review

Page 136. Activity 1: especially—adverb; explains how the tortoise was invited; little short—adjectives; describe the tortoise's legs; seized—verb; tells the action of the tortoise

Page 137. Activity 2: 1. teeth; I; 2. weddings; R; 3. birds; R; 4. grounds; R; Activity 3: 1. attitude; 2. compassion; 3. Astonishment

Stop and Think! Units 7–8 Understand

Pages 140–141. 1. The stork is angry at the fox for tricking him with the food; 2. Anansi makes Turtle believe that he will get food, then he tricks him into washing his hands so that he misses the meal; 3. The food was underwater and he was too light, so he floated to the top; 4. In stanza 3, the reader discovers that Anansi is greedy and doesn't plan on really feeding hungry Turtle. This leads to Turtle tricking him back; 5. Answers will vary. Sample responses for both stories: Don't play tricks unless you want the same treatment. When you try to outsmart someone, you may be the one outsmarted; 6. Answers will vary; 7. The picture shows the action that is happening between the fox and the stork. The first picture shows the fox tricking the stork and the second shows the stork tricking the fox again; 8. Answers will vary. Sample responses: water, food spread on the table, expressions on the characters' faces.